Israeli Mythogynies

SUNY Series in Modern Jewish Literature and Culture

Sarah Blacher Cohen, Editor

ISRAELI MYTHOGYNIES

Women in Contemporary Hebrew Fiction

ESTHER FUCHS

State University of New York Press

Published by
State University of New York Press, Albany

For information, address State University of New York
Press, State University Plaza, Albany, N.Y., 12246

Library of Congress Cataloging in Publication Data

Fuchs, Esther, 1953-
    Israeli mythogynies.

    (SUNY series in modern Jewish literature and culture)
    Includes index.
    1. Israeli fiction—History and criticism.
2. Women in literature.   I. Title.   II. Series.
PJ5030.W65F83   1987   892.4′36′080352042 86-14433
ISBN 0-88706-417-5
ISBN 0-88706-418-3 (pbk.)

10 9 8 7 6 5 4 3 2 1

Contents

CONTENTS

Preface

The distance between Jerusalem and the American East Coast is considerable, yet shuttling between conferences on Hebrew literature and on women's studies over the past five years has seemed more like an interstellar enterprise. The time warp was no less dramatic when I traveled from Boston, the permanent site of the Jewish Studies Association to the various cities that hosted the annual conventions of the Modern Language Association. What was taken for granted by one audience seemed outrageous or foreign to another. To a certain extent, this book is the product of my shuttling between Hebrew literary critics and feminist critics. To the former I had to justify my interest in gender as a category of literary analysis, and to the latter I often had to explain the value of Hebrew literature as a unique study, while to myself I was trying to explain the phenomenon of different scholarly subjectivities.

Traveling through epistemological time can be frustrating, but it is also revealing. I can say with certainty that my struggle with this project dramatized for me one of the fundamental premises of this book: that value is often contingent on the existence of an interpretive community. It confirmed my belief that perspective determines not only the interpretation but the shape of experience, in other words, that the text is in the reader. Working on Hebrew literature in an Anglo American and French frame of reference and working on women in a Hebrew frame of reference also allowed me to experience on an academic level what it means to be an Other. What was perhaps most revealing was to discover how difficult it is to part ways with my mentors and teachers and to criticize books I have grown to love.

The obstacles I had to face in my study of women in Israeli fiction forced me to extend the critical agendas and literary terminology that were available to me in both Hebrew and feminist criticism when I first began this study. I had to introduce new words into the feminist literary vocabulary and new analytic concepts into current Hebrew literary language. In attempting to explain to myself the status of feminist criticism within the academic environment, I learned more than I expected about the oppressive power of conventional wisdom and about the subtle but real relationships between sexual politics and academic politics. In attempting to clarify the uniqueness and value of modern Hebrew literature, I came to appreciate the need for a culture-specific perspective in feminist literary theory. I began to attend to the impact of state politics on literary presentations of women and to the continuities as well as transformations in male and female works.

I never thought that one day I would be able to thank those who asked me why I chose this subject. Now that I wrestled with the premises of this question and realized how much it has taught me about the politics of knowledge, I can extend my thanks. But I would especially like to acknowledge the helpful questions of students and faculty that made this project into the challenging intellectual adventure it often was. For their interest and encouraging response, I am grateful to the members of the Feminist Research Colloquia at the University of Texas and at the University of Arizona. For their intelligent comments on the entire manuscript, I thank the anonymous readers as well as Elizabeth Abel, Susan Aiken, Sarah Blacher Cohen, Sidra DeKoven Ezrahi, and Jane Marcus who read and commented on parts of previous drafts. The support of Dafna N. Izraeli and the staff of *Noqa* was inspiring. With them, I hope to see this book published in Hebrew.

CHAPTER 1

Introduction

Feminist criticism has so proliferated in the last decade and a half, and there is so much energy and creativity in the field that theoreticians are faced with increasing difficulties in finding a consensual definition for its various projects. Recent anthologies such as *The New Feminist Criticism, Making a Difference, The Female Body in Western Culture, Gender and Reading* and *The [M]other Tongue* attest to the methodological variety and the growing theoretical complexity of the field.[1] The fresh insights and revolutionary questioning feminist critics have brought to time-honored canons and forgotten texts may only be rivaled by the deep impact they made on the best literary minds and most progressive academic institutions of our time. This is not to say that these achievements were easily won. Nina Auerbach, for example, argues that feminist critics in the Anglo-American academe continue to be more tolerated than understood, "more appeased than listened to, more pigeonholed than read."[2] For a Hebrew critic like myself, working in a field that has barely taken notice of the existence of feminist criticism, the prospects of being "tolerated" and "appeased" elicit vague longings, even envy. For what Hebrew feminist critics must contend with at this point is at best ignorance, at worst subtle resistance.

In *On Deconstruction*, Culler argues that: "Criticism based on the presumption of continuity between the reader's experience and a woman's experience and on a concern with images of women is likely to become most forceful as a critique of the phallocentric assumptions that govern literary works. This critique is by now a familiar genre, authoritatively established. . ."[3] Culler must surely have in mind an Anglo-American or French temporality, for in Hebrew literary-critical time, "by now" "this feminist critique" is neither "familiar" nor "authoritatively established." In Hebrew literary time, "by now," thirty-seven years after the publication of Simone de Beauvoir's *The Second Sex*

1

and seventeen years after the publication of Kate Millet's *Sexual Politics*, "this feminist critique" is the name of a freak phenomenon. There is no feminist interpretive community in the field of Hebrew literature, which is why critics interested in this kind of reading have "as of now" no legitimacy. Excepting a few anthologies of works by lesser known women authors and contemporary poets, and a handful of articles, the feminist revolution in literary schlolarship seems to have taken place on a different planet.[4]

The dismissive attitude toward feminist criticism within the field of Hebrew literature reveals among other things the androcentric perspective of the literary critics who at present dominate the field. It exposes the cultural agendas of a gender-blind criticism that presents itself as objective or pluralistic. Needless to say, genuine pluralism or objectivity would make it impossible for critics who profess it to preclude *any* approach to the text as 'illegitimate.' The obliviousness to the important contributions of feminist criticism suggests among other things that a gender-blind approach to the literary text disguises a set of evaluative priorities inspired by cultural norms rather than universal verities.

But how can we explain the ignorance of feminist criticism within an otherwise sophisticated academic community, boasting among other achievements the internationally known Tel Aviv School of Poetics and the literary journal *Ha-Sifrut*? A possible clue for this riddle lies in what Benjamin Harshaw, the founder of the Tel Aviv School of poetics decried as "the stunning conservativeness of the literary establishment in this lively state (i.e., Israel), its fundamental misunderstanding of the differences between an academic approach and journalistic impressionistic approaches, between research and criticism and high-school instruction."[5] Though Harshaw is basically right in his observations, the terms of his critique betray the prroblems that are at present haunting the "academic approach" and the "research and scholarship" he implicitly endorses. For the binary opposition between research and impressionistic criticism implies a belief in the former's invulnerability to subjective and ideological bias. The fallacy of this alleged invulnerability has been forcefully exposed by feminist critics both implicitly and explicitly.[6] An academic elite that continues to endorse the scientific model as the right approach to the literary text will naturally balk at the political implications of feminist criticism.[7] The paradox is that by remaining impervious to the male bias underlying the selection and definition of their scholarly projects, those who would like to think of themselves as literary scientists are betraying their own ideals. For, as Evelyn Fox Keller points out, feminist criticism is dedicated to the eradication of bias in the same way that genuine science must be.[8]

One might speculate that the academic resistance to feminist criticism is partly inspired by the popular hostility in Israel towards the women's movement. Since its establishment in 1972 by Marcia Freedman, who was temporarily elected to the Knesset, the movement has drawn nervous and suspicious responses.[9] The movement's opponents have argued that its concerns are American and inapplicable to the needs of an egalitarian state like Israel. The endorsement of these popular attitudes within the academe is to say the least strange. It is strange because scholars are expected to be critical of popular generalizations rather than succumb to them. Academicians are supposed to judge critical theories in accordance to their potential analytic effectiveness and suggestiveness, not by their national provenance or popular appeal. If feminist criticism is unacceptable because it is 'American,' how do we explain the happy reception by Hebrew critics of theories generated by American New Criticism, the Prague School, Russian Formalism or French Structuralism?

The relatively late arrival of New Critical and Formalist theories to the Hebrew literary scene may provide us with yet another explanation for the resistance of the Hebrew literary academy to feminist, or for that matter all political criticism. The hegemony of the aestheticist and scientific metaphors in what I might call the center of the Israeli critical polysystem during the 1960s and early 1970s may be the result of New Critical rebellion against the socialist realist platforms of the Palmah Generation (late 1940s-late 1950s). Yael Feldman speculates that "the Israeli indifference to political criticism stems from the relentless pressures and inescapable presence of politics in daily Israeli life:" It is their *fear* of the overpowering presence of political issues, palpable as they are in the Israeli experience, that endows the scientific metaphor with such alluring power. The delusion of rationality and objectivity is, no doubt, a greatly needed defense against the turbulent reality of Israeli life (italics in the original).[10] Be it as it may, the fastidious insistence on separating politics from poetics began to give in the mid 1970s, perhaps as a result of the Yom Kippur War of 1973. By the late 1970s several critical surveys began to emphasize the mimetic, experiential and political aspects of contemporary Hebrew writing.[11]

The new recognition of the inseparability of life and art, remains limited to an androcentric perspective. "Experience" in the new theories means male experience, "politics" refers to the procedures of male ruled governments and male dominated parties. A quick glance at recent theories about contemporary Israeli fiction reveals that most of them tend to marginalize or altogether ignore female experience and female writing. Though female authors like Amalia Kahana-Carmon, Yehudith

Hendel, Naomi Fraenkel, Shulamith Har-Even, Rachel Eytan, and more recently Ruth Almog, Yael Medini, Hadara Lazar and Ariela Deem published prose-fiction throughout the 1970s, their works have rarely been incorporated in male-produced theoretical surveys of the late 1970s and early 1980s. Accusing Amalia Kahana-Carmon of "pridefulness, banality, intellectualism and narrow-mindedness," and dismissing her triptych *Magnetic fields* (1978) as a "literary accident," the important critic, Dan Miron grounds his critical model of Israeli fiction in the late 1970s in an all-male model.[12] But while Miron focuses specifically on the literary productions of 1978, Yosef Oren presumes to give us a much more inclusive survey of trends in Israeli fiction of the 1970s without as much as mentioning a woman author.[13] Does this mean that Hebrew women authors have had nothing useful to say about "experience" or about Israeli actualities? Or does this mean that their work does not lend itself easily to the androcentric paradigms postulated by the critics? It seems to me that the best answer is to be found in the traditional association in Hebrew letters of significant creativity with masculinity. In the words of Amalia Kahana-Carmon, the most a woman author in Hebrew letters can aspire to is "to be a complementary phenomenon and a helpmate alongside the mainstream of the literature. [She is allowed to be] a partner—yes, but not the thing itself."[14]

A myopic political vision which focuses exclusively on male-produced works and on male subjects as national symbols is just as inimical to the development of a radical inquiry of literary epistemologies and the political assumptions underlying them as the restrictive use of the term "politics." In Hebrew literary criticism this term defines such issues as national security, the Arab-Israeli conflict, party politics, ethnic and social conflicts or the various aspects of Zionism. The concept of sexual politics in the sense of the power relations between the sexes or the concept of political criticism aimed at the complicity of literary trends and hegemonic ideologies is alien to most critics. Thus for example, in a recent article, Gershon Shaked, a major Hebrew scholar argues, without defining what he means by "political" that: "Any writer, certainly any writer of Hebrew fiction during the 1970s and 1980s, can be the object of political questions."[15] What Shaked means is that contemporary Hebrew fiction often struggles with Israel's political and social problems. The "challenges and question marks" invoked in Shaked's title do not describe the critic's challenge to the literary canon or to normative literary discourse, but the author's challenge to the sociopolitical status quo.

The predictable result of such a critical awareness of literature's political dimension is yet another hymnological affirmation of the contemporary Hebrew canon. As Shaked put it: "It is characteristic of good literature [and of all good art] that it does not approve of the existing pattern of society. Just as it wishes to overturn accepted forms, so it also attempts to change outlooks through the model it creates. The whole point of literature lies in this attitude of opposition, and this is particularly so in Israel in the seventies and eighties, where everything cries out for the opposite."[16] But if the great contemporary Hebrew canon is by definition oppositional, where does this leave the feminist critic who argues that there is a complicity between the Hebrew canon and "the existing pattern of society," especially where sexual politics is concerned? the argument that all great literature is oppositional implies that the task of the truly great critic is to detect this opposition and applaud it. In other words, great critics are expected to do the opposite of what great authors do. Feminist critics who challenge the present shape of the Hebrew canon, the evaluative systems that underlie its formation, and the narrow scope of the world it represents must be perceived in this context as noncritics. Their questions are nonquestions, the observations irrelevant, their discourse nonliterary, their concerns illicit. What is currently understood in Hebrew criticism as political criticism is political indeed, but not in the sense it is usually understood. It is political rather in that it polices the "proper" rules for practicing literary criticism. It is political in that its implicit emphasis on traditional androcentric concerns categorizes the feminist critic as a second class citizen in the literary critical community.[17]

One might presume that *all* critical projects pointing up the complicity of literature with hegemonic ideologies would not be welcome in the Hebrew critical establishment. Yet, this is not quite the case. Special allowances are made for critics concerned with recognized or privileged Others. Critics who question the ideological presumptions underlying literary representations of, for example, Jews, or the connections between Jewish identity and writing are considered as 'mainstream' scholars. Similarly, critics who question the representation of Arabs in Hebrew literature, or of Sephardim in both Sephardic and Ashkenazic literature find it unnecessary to defend their methodological procedures or theoretical premises. Within the context of modern Hebrew criticism national/ethinc identity is perceived as a privileged subject and, consequently, critics working on related issues will be exempt from defending or even explaining the literary value or relevance of their projects.[18]

It is clear then that what we might call relevance or significance are products of conventions rather than inherent value. To the extent that relevance is legislated by cultural conventions, it is a political rather than a literary issue. There is no logical reason why leading Hebrew literary

critics should value the debunking of Jewish stereotypes while dismissing as irrelevant the scholarly questioning of female stereotypes. There
is obviously no literary justification for the privileging of ethnonational
identity over psychosexual identity. Literary critics who are aware of
the vulnerability of even great authors and critics to anti-Semitic
ideologies should also be aware—or at least let themselves become
aware—of a similar vulnerability of the literary/critical text to
misogynous ideologies. As I said, however, this is not the case in
mainstream Hebrew literary circles. Most critics, especially those who
are interested in the national metaphor, tend to dismiss as marginal the
sexual metaphor. Most of them perceive only the former as a
political sign; sexual politics (the power relations between the sexes)
is a foreign concept to the best critics in the field. This is the
case among major Hebrew critics in both Israel and in the United
States.

The emphasis of leading American trained critics on nationalist symbolism in the study of Hebrew literature might be symptomatic of their
(unconscious?) attempt to 'prove' the relevance of the field to scholars of
more privileged areas of Jewish scholarship, e.g. Bible, Rabbinics, Jewish
history and Jewish philosophy. Be it as it may, the national-allegorical interpretation of Israeli narratives has become so dominant, that attention
to mimetic dimensions, like sexuality and sexual politics, interpersonal
and intersexual conflict and relationships—topics that make up the
thematic grid of most Israeli literature—has become suspect unless properly 'contextualized' within the 'broader' (i.e., national) scheme of
things. This is not to say that allegorical references to the nation/state
are not embedded in many Israeli love stories. As I show in this book,
there is very often a thematic or symbolic interlacing of erotic and national themes in Israeli literature. For example, neurotic heterosexual
relations often signify the degenerative aspect of Israel's wars with its
neighbors, while descriptions of war enhance the private wars between
sexual partners. Yet our awareness of one metaphor does not have to
eclipse the other. The privileging of the national metaphor at the expense of the sexual one is to say the least restrictive if not distortive.

In an essay entitled "The Kidnapping of Bialik and Tchernichovsky,"
Rober Alter, a leading scholar of Hebrew literature in the United States,
rightly criticized the reductive emphasis on the national aspect of these
poets' work.[19] Like his Israeli counterparts, Alter challenged the
obsessive concern with the the national meaning of even the most personal poems. Yet throughout the 1970s and increasingly in the 1980s this
kind of "kidnapping" has been the order of the day among American
trained critics. Expanding Halkin's vision of Hebrew literature as a

primarily national literature, numerous leading critics have been focusing almost exclusively on the national meaning of contemporary Israeli fiction.[20] Alter himself wrote in 1977 that: "One of the most striking qualities of Israeli literature since the beginning of the 1960s and, increasingly into the 1970's, is that it remains intensely, almost obsessively, national in its concerns while constantly pressing to address itself to universal situations, perhaps to an international audience as well."[21] The problem is that the "national" and "universal" concerns addressed by most Hebrew critics hinge on male protagonists, just as their critical theories are grounded in all male authored models. For example, Shimon Sandbank in his discussion of new developments in contemporary fiction mentions Amalia Kahana-Carmon as a critic of Amos Oz, while ignoring her fiction and that of other female authors.[22]

Readers who would turn to American anthologies of Hebrew Israeli fiction will quickly conclude that Hebrew women authors do not exist. For not only do American anthologizers tend to omit Hebrew women authors from their collections, they also fail to acknowledge or explain their omissions. Such procedures easily create the impression that if Israeli women authors exist, they are not as good as their male counterparts. How else are we to interpret such titles as "Israeli Stories: A Selection of the Best Writing in Israel Today" or "Eight Great Hebrew Short Novels," which are only two samples of exclusively male literary selections?"[23] In his preface to the all-male anthology he co-edited, Alan Lelchuk explains that he was guided by "the literary merit" and the "literary qualities" of his selections.[24] Since Lelchuk does not bother to explain his criteria for literary merit or quality, we are implicitly invited to assume that such evaluative terms are to be taken for granted. The omission of women-authored short novels implies further that only male authors have written "great" short novels in Hebrew.

What is subtly implied by the dismissive treatment of women authors in the Hebrew literary academy was recently explicitly expressed by the well-known poet David Avidan in a recent commentary on the poetry of Yona Wallach. Avidan asserts that Wallach was not worthy of the critical assessments of her work which filled the Israeli literary press shortly after her death."[25] Avidan is especially disturbed by the critical reviews which evaluated Wallach as one of the greatest Hebrew poets of the twentieth century. He argues that it is erroneous to consider Wallach as one of the greatest poets, because she was after all a *woman poet*. We might be correct, according to Avidan, in considering her as one of the best *women poets*. Since, however, there were only few women poets to compete against, Wallach may not have been such a great poet after all. Avidan is trying to remind us of the superiority of male poets (himself in-

cluded) by devaluing female poetry. By appealing to Wallach's female
sex, he demands that critics reconsider their evaluation of Wallach, an
evaluation which appears to threaten male contenders to the status of
poetic greatness. Among other things, Avidan assures us that Wallach
failed to become a [male] poet, although she wished to be considered
one.

In my response to Avidan's comments, I pointed out his phallocratic
assumptions about the alleged supremacy of male writing. I pointed out
the inconsistencies in his arguments, and the androcentric prejudice
which inspired his denial of Wallach's greatness.[26] Avidan's response to
my comments dramatized for me the hopelessness of entering into a
dialogue with phallocrats. Basically, Avidan repeated his a priori judgment about the superiority of male writing, declaring that he does not
know why "the male mind functions higher and upwards and the female
mind downwards and to the breadth."[27] Avidan's allusion to the male
phallus (higher, upwards) as the source of male poetic supremacy
reveals the unconscious biologism and unimaginative conventionalism of
androcentric authors and critics who are not as willing as Avidan to
advertise their prejudices. By constructing a metaphorical binary opposition between masculine verticality and feminine horizontality, Avidan
believes he has proved the former's superiority. But even if we were to
accept his infantile biologization of male poetry, why is breadth and
depth less important in poetic production than upward protrusiveness?

There is, however, an additional factor which may explain the
resistance of both Israeli and Anglo-American critics to feminist
criticism. To put it bluntly, modern Hebrew literature is still struggling
for a wider recognition than its relatively small readership can offer.
Modern Hebrew fiction has come into its own only since the turn of the
century, its history is shorter and its canon less stable than its Anglo-
American or continental counterparts. A feminist critique of the
phallocentric excesses of D.H. Lawrence, Norman Mailer, or Henry
Miller may perhaps be unsettling, just as a critique of Montherland,
Claudel or Breton might be, but it will not be as *threatening* as a feminist
critique of major authors of modern Hebrew literature. Because a
radical feminist inquiry is likely to point up the evaluative contingencies
underlying the formation of the canon, Hebrew critics may be more
defensive about the "correct" critical approach to literature than their
counterparts in other countries.

At this point, the feminist critic in Hebrew literature is an Other, one
who is both alien and dismissible.[28] As a mythical construct she shares
the characteristics of the Hebrew female author and the male-created
female character. Like them she seems to pursue the wrong goals, and
like them, she is concerned with trivialities. Like them she represents a

frightening deviation from the male norm, or the Self. Like her fictional counterparts she lurks at the outskirts of patriarchal order ready to destroy its most cherished values. Her presence, like that of the Hebrew female author seems like an impudent intrusion into the all male club of civilized literary discourse. The female Other is an irritant which must be expelled or ignored. Male authors often present her as lacking consciousness, and/or conscience. Male critics attempt to domesticate her fictions, interpret them in accordance with the Self's vision, or deny them any importance.

Yet, for all her objectionability, the female Other is vital for the survival of patriarchy. To a culture that associates meaning with masculinity, there is something profoundly reassuring in the patriarchal myth[s] of womanhood or what I define in this book as "mythogyny." The image of the Other exempts patriarchal thinking from articulating the meaning and implications of sexual difference. It permits the hegemonic value system to project on the female Other what it idolizes and condemns. This is why patriarchal mythogynies thrive on the facile interpretations of sexual differences as bipolar dichotomies, such as spirit/matter, culture/nature, activity/passivity. As we shall see in chapter 2, the symbolic pole assigned to woman varies according to the shifts in the hegemonic evaluations of these symbols. Authors also differ from each other in their mythogynous constructions, as we shall see in chapters 3 and 4. What remains the same is the association of female characters with whatever is defined in the specific work as Other.

The stunning parallels between the status of the female character and that of the author speak to the effectiveness of gender as a category of literary analysis. For as we shall see, these parallels transcend the traditional boundaries that separate the text from the author and both from the reader. But even as we are made aware of the fluid boundaries between social and fictional constructions of womanhood, we must not lose sight of the fact that unlike the androcentric representations of womanhood, or what I call here "gyniconologies," Israeli female writers do speak back. As we shall see, the most forceful challenge to traditional mythogynies were generated not by the shift from the Palmah Generation to the generation of Statehood, but by the innovative revisions of Amalia Kahana-Carmon, the first woman author to have gained broad recognition in Hebrew literature, notwithstanding her controversial poetics. As we shall see in chapters 5 and 6, Kahana-Carmon's revisionary writing—what I term in this book "gynography"—subtly parodies the patriarchal mythogynies of her male predecessors and contemporaries. While often drawing on traditional gyniconologies, she often reinterprets them in unexpected and as yet unrecognized ways.

It should be clear, by now, that what I am interested in is not the extent to which Israeli mythogynies prevaricate historical realities or authentic experiences of Israeli women.[29] Rather, I read Israeli mythogynies as ideological expressivities. To gauge the interactions of patriarchal norms with changing poetic, social and nationalist ideologies, I examine the denotational, connotational and symbolic aspects of pervasive gyniconologies.[30] The denotational aspect refers to the relationship between a specific female image and its human-like referent. In this context I am combining mimetic and functional approaches to literary characterization.[31] Mimetically, I refer to the female character as "woman" and consider the domestic and social roles (wife, lover), as well as the psychological traits attributed to her. Functionally, the character is considered for its uses as, for example, the foil of the male protagonist, his antagonist, or the catalyst of his actions. The connotational aspect of common gyniconologies is concerned with what the latter imply about womanhood in general. Repeated representations of female characters as mad or passive, for example, are considered as partial manifestations of traditional ideologies about female otherness. The symbolic aspect of the gyniconologies I shall discuss refers to their relationship to abstract concepts like the land, society, or the state. In this context, I shall ask why certain abstract concepts are gynomorphized (or portrayed as female) in certain periods and in particular works. I shall also speculate on some of the meanings of the repeated gynomorphization of certain abstract concepts in the context of national and sexual politics.

In chapter 2, I study the gyniconological continuities and transformations from the Palmah Generation to the Generation of Statehood. Focusing mostly on the connotational and symbolic aspects of male-authored gyniconologies, I am studying the relationship between the latter and the social and aesthetic trends that have shaped the fiction of the 1960s and the 1970s. The increasingly forbidding female images are studied here in the context of Israel's political (in the traditional sense of foreign affairs, national security) crisis, and shifts in ideological and aesthetic hegemonies. The new aesthetic philosophies of the Generation of Statehood will be especially central to my discussion of gyniconological transformations as they shed much light on the emerging tendency to gynomorphize the various objects of the social critique, be it the land, the state or the increasingly capitalistic society. Despite my attention to transformative trends, I remain attentive to the unchanging aspects of the most pervasive gyniconologies in the major male-authored works of the 1960s and 1970s,

In chapters 3 and 4, I examine the mythogynies of two of Israel's most celebrated and influential writers, A.B. Yehoshua, and Amos Oz. My analytical method here is to compare mimetically and functionally female with male characters. In chapter 3, I follow a thematic ordering, while in chapter 4, I use a chronological one, studying various gyniconologies rather than thematic categories within the context of a particular work. While neither Yehoshua nor Oz can be said to resist patriarchal doctrines, they differ in the ways they apply them to the different mythogynies they create. My discussion of the authors' respective political and aesthetic ideologies is meant to illuminate these differences.

Continuities and transformations are the hidden motifs of chapters 2 through 4 and in important ways they also give shape to chapters 5 and 6 which are dedicated to the landmark work of Amalia Kahana-Carmon who, unlike her male counterparts, is little known outside of Israel. For despite her creative revisions of patriarchal mythogynies, her gynographies are to some extent continuous with them. Nevertheless, as we shall see, Kahana-Carmon's gynographic revisions are more substantive than the innovative gyniconologies offered by the New Wave of the early 1960s. In chapter 5, I suggest among other things that Kahana-Carmon's much debated poetics must be understood in a gynographic framework, and that it is within this framework that we can better understand the ambialent critical responses to her work. In chapter 6, I offer a detailed study of Kahana-Carmon's revisionary treatment of a traditional mythogyny about a confined and alienated housewife. Beyond its specific objects of analysis, my comparative study of Kahana-Carmon's Mrs. Talmor and Amos Oz's Mrs. Gonen is intended to serve as a heuristic approach to gyniconological relationships between male- and female-authored mythogynies.

Most Hebrew literary scholars would probably agree that the value of Hebrew literature in its various phases, lies in its remarkable ability to challenge the ideologies that inspired it. To the extent that Hebrew literature never stopped challenging the social and political movements that brought it into existence, it never ceased to be in some sense radical. To the extent that modern Hebrew writers continue to struggle with glib popular interpretations of social reality, and to offer alternatives to predominant epistemologies and societal hegemonies they are revolutionaries. As a student of modern Hebrew literature, I was often made aware of the iconoclastic zeal of the *maskilim*, the secularist intellectuals who rebelled against the Jewish European ghetto in the eighteenth and nineteenth centuries. I learned to respect the audacious rebellion of the *Tehiya*, or modern Hebraic Renaissance movement of the turn of the century against cultural assimilation. With other critics of contemporary Hebrew literature, I have been impressed with the continued questioning of Israeli society by the best authors of the Palmah Generation and the contemporary Generation of Statehood. This radical heritage makes it all the more urgent for students and critics of Hebrew literature to question the strange complicity of major Hebrew fiction with one of the most oppressive ideologies of all times—patriarchy.

CHAPTER 2

The Generation of Statehood: Gyniconological Transformations and Continuities

In the late 1950s and early 1960s, the canonic center of the literary polysystem began to accommodate literary expressivities that have been marginalized in previous decades.[1] Experimental, phantasmatic, and confessional styles began to edge out the socialist-realistic platform of the Palmah Generation, which dominated the literary canon from the late 1940s to the late 1950s. Literary historians and New Critics alike were quick to record with varying degrees of approval an apparent thematic shift from the "engaged" writing to one that emphasizes artistic sophistication.[2] The new focus on the universal parameters of the personal and subjective experience became the most valued distinction of what came to be know as the "New Wave," the vanguard of the Generation of Statehood.

With the new focus, critical attention shifted from the social realism of most of the Palmah authors to the esoteric parables of A.B. Yehoshua, the archetypalism of Amos Oz, the lyricism of Aharon Appelfeld, the autobiographical allegories of Pinhas Sadeh, the stream of consciousness of Amalia Kahana-Carmon, and the phantasmatic fiction of David Shahar. The increasingly academic readership now expected that fiction would fulfil the artistic prerequisites laid down by the New Criticism. Thus, even authors like A.B. Yehoshua and Amos Oz, who were otherwise involved in national politics, made an effort to be as circumlocutious as possible in their references to Israeli society. Allegorical ambiguity became the order of the day. As we shall see, more often than not, what served as an allegorical substitute for what many of the New Wave authors saw as a degenerating society were gyniconologies of mad, materialistic, and hedonistic women bent on the destruction of the male protagonist, or the national Self.

The apparent flight from Israeli reality was especially pronounced in the early phase of the New Wave and began to taper off towards the late 1960s, especially after the Six Days War in 1967. Yet, not until the mid 1970s, probably in the wake of the Yom Kippur War of 1973, do we note the beginnings of a trend which might be defined as a "new realism." Critics like Dan Miron see this phenomenon as the product of an effort to combine a mimetic representation of collective and subjective experiences.[3]

In addition to the influence of Virginia Woolf, D.H. Lawrence, Franz Kafka, Thomas Mann, William Faulkner, Henry Miller, and Albert Camus, the New Wave responded to the irony of S.Y. Agnon, the mythic world of M.Y. Berdichevsky, and the lyricism of U.N. Gnessin. The omniscient narrator of the Palmah Generation was replaced by an unreliable narrator, and the martial or moral hero, by an inept, isolated anti-hero. Authorial identification with the protagonist's point of view gave way to ironic distance, and the etiological plot to an open-ended or circular one.

The eclipse of the Palmah Generation is closely related to the loss of the Labor Movement's ideological hegemony, which was largely caused by the perceived incongruity between the Labor Movement's idealistic principles and the government's realpolitik. The intellectual elite condemned the Sinai Campaign of 1956 as a worthless war, the economic recession of the late 1950s as an antiproletarian measure, and the state's politics of pragmatism in general as a betrayal of the pioneering spirit. The Westernization of the state and its perceived failure to become the exclusive center of the Jewish nation was perceived as a betrayal of Zionism. The repeated confrontations with the Arabs were criticized as violating the pacifist and humanitarian goals of Labor Zionism and were often diagnosed as suicidal ventures or as the outcome of an inescapable historical fate, dooming Jews to perpetual alienation and rejection.

Although still upheld by the majority of the native intellectual elite, the previously hegemonic socialist value system was eroded by the transition to an industrialized capitalistic economy and a mostly urban and bureaucratized society. The center of the cultural polysystem shifted from a revolutionary ethos to a middle-class traditionalism, shared by both East European and Middle Eastern immigrants, who soon became the majority of the new population.

   The political and artistic perspective of the Generation of Statehood did not change, however, the old double standard: female characters in the male-authored fiction of the 1960s and 1970s are not only more visible but also more sinister. For while the emphasis on personal experience dignified to some extent representations of domesticity and its traditional association with femininity, the interest in subjective experience remained almost exclusively identified with masculinity. Now that masculinity was no longer associated with the extradomestic environment of the kibbutz or the military, it became necessary to reformulate traditional mythogynies. Yet, as we shall see, instead of challenging the Otherness which typified Palmah mythognynies, most of the male authors of the Generation of Statehood preferred to replace the old dichotomy (public/private) with new ones (spirit/matter; culture/nature) that still favored the masculine.

   Since the new, self-absorbed, alienated, sensitive, and tormented male hero began to be defined in opposition to the public realm, a new thematic alignment between that realm and the female Other had to be established if the underlying hierarchical male/female dichotomy was to be maintained. In addition to the feminine gender of the Hebrew word for 'society' (hevra), what facilitated the new emphasis on woman as the symbolic signifier of society was the traditional association of women with procreativity, social survival with genealogical continuity and the domestic sphere. But if the Palmah's domestic gyniconologies sometimes serve as idealized symbolizations of peace (as in S. Yizhar's fiction), in the New Wave, they assume increasingly lurid connotations.

   For one thing, in the Generation of Statehood, society becomes the symbolic locus of corruption and spiritual stagnation. The association of society with the domestic, feminine realm therefore means that the male hero flees not only from social restrictions but also from femininity. While woman frustrates the male hero's attempt to join the collective, in the Palmah fiction of (Aharon Megged, Nathan Shaham, or Yigal Mossinsohn), in the New Wave she obstructs his attempt to flee from society. Yet, because of the important shift in the evaluation of the collective experience, the implications of these apparently different gyniconologies remain largely the same. In both roles, woman obstructs the male hero's way to freedom and self-actualization. Male-authored mythogynies in both generations deny woman the ability to share the male hero's confusion, existential ennui, or social alienation. Male-authored gyniconologies of the Generation of Statehood continue to separate femininity from the mimetic evocation of conscience, and consciousness. Restricted to the role of wife or lover, male-authored gyniconologies seem to endorse the idea that women are incapable of doubting, regretting, questioning, suffering, or meaningfully creating. Just as national dilemmas are pondered in the Palmah fiction by male heroes, so is existential angst the exclusive preserve of the new anti-hero. Male-authored mythogynies in both generations seem to marginalize with equal virtuosity what we might call "female humanhood" and to trivialize the specificities of the female condition, or womanhood.

If in the Palmah literature the average female character is condemned for her individualism, in the Generation of Statehood she tends to be condemned for her overattachment to the life of the masses. If the heroic quest in the Palmah fiction (as in Moshe Shamir and Yigal Mossinsohn) leads away from woman to an ideal community, in the Generation of Statehood this quest takes the male hero away from both matter and society in his quest for meaning; in other words, he must transcend his relationships with women.

The male-authored fiction of the Generation of Statehood reformulates female Otherness without challenging the hierarchical dichotomy which excludes woman from the human sphere of volition and action. The new mythogynies associate women with the most objectionable aspects of the emerging urbanite, industrialized, and militarized society. Drawing on age-old stereotypes which typecast women as embodiments of materialism, hedonism, and corruption, the Generation of Statehood—notably the allegorists—began to generate gyniconologies of female Otherness in the social, psychological, sexual, and national sense. The new female Other is materialistic and selfish, steeped in meaningless consumerist pursuits. She is not merely neurotic like her male counterpart, but constitutionally mad. She is oversexed, adulterous, and profligate. Unlike her male counterparts, her need for sex is purely biological and symptomatic of hedonism or narcissism. She is also often a foreigner who is largely detached from the primary concerns of national survival. She often emerges as a national enemy who secretly hopes for the destruction of the male national Self.[4]

The increasing visibility of female characters in male-authored fiction by the Generation of Statehood is closely related to the growing emphasis on sex as a primary principle of characterization. But the new sexual explicitness has only increased the stereotyping of women as sex objects on the one hand and as nymphomaniacs on the other. Despite the emphasis on a thematic area which has largely been taboo in previous decades, the traditional double standard which praises in men what it condemns in women, continues to inspire sexual gyniconologies. While male characters pursue sex in the attempt to either flee social oppression or to attain a transcendent truth, women indulge in sex because it is their nature to do so. When it is not objectified, female sexuality emerges in male-created mythogynies as a kind of perversion. But in her capacity as both sex object and nymphomaniac, the female Other is a manifestation of matter. In this sense, woman's sexuality dovetails with her materialism, hedonism, formless mind, lack of conscience and consciousness, and indifference to the nation's predicament or other ideals.

Perhaps the most dramatic break with the Palmah tradition has been achieved in the fiction of Pinhas Sadeh. Against the socialist, realist platform of the Palmah Generation, Sadeh posits a mystical and explicitly allegorical poetics. His heroic protagonist searches for meaning in christological narratives and European brothels rather than in the kibbutz, the army, or the family. While the previous model hero struggles to break out of the confined limits of his private world to realize the higher goals of the ideal community, Sadeh's hero struggles to break away from the confines of society and to plunge into the mystery of the Self and the Universe through artistic creativity. Yet, like his Palmah counterpart, Sadeh's protagonist is an idealized hero who invites identification and admiration. Most significantly, as in the Palmah literature, the heroic stature of the protagonist is directly related to his ability to conquer or transcent the female Other.

In *Life as a Parable* (1959) Sadeh's narrator-protagonist rejects both the carnal women for whom he lusts (Adah, Havah, Sarah, Abigail) and the beautiful women he loves (Yaelah, Ayalah, his wife Y.) as material obstacles to his way to self-realization and artistic perfection. If, as a carnal Lilith, woman drags the hero down to "the sewers" of the flesh, she is doubly dangerous as a beloved Eve, for she lures the hero to love "the mundane thing in itself." As the hero puts it: "The times I spent loving the mundane thing in itself (as when I was living with the beautiful Ayalah, or when I was married), for its character and quality, for the happiness it gave me, these times were spiritually dead, times of true sin."[5] The carnal woman must be left behind because through her the hero might give in to the temptations of the flesh; the beloved woman must be left behind, because through her he may yield to the mundane bliss of domestic life, and thus be devoured by "the infernal dogs of civil life, hypocrisy, the masses, the family, civilization, money, job and the state."[6]

If the hero of *Life as a Parable* uses his romantic and sexual liaisons with women as stairs leading up to his self-styled spiritual heaven, Absalom, the hero of *On the Human Condition* (1967), has no apparent use for women at all. Worshipped by his adolescent sister, Abigail, a sublime combination of the virgin Mary and a desexed Beatrice, Absalom is free to meditate on God and to write poetry without being unduly distracted by "the mundane thing itself." As a breathtaking manifestation of nature's naked beauty, Abigail herself is incapable of artistic creativity or original thinking. The only mental ability she appears to command is mnemonic. Having memorized Absalom's poems and spontaneous reflections about life, Abigail recites them throughout the novel, thus serving as a convenient foil whose major function is to enhance the genius of her brother. Absalom is as superior to Abigail as culture is to nature, as the beautiful spirit is to the beautiful body. Sadeh's mythogynies are worthy of attention because, despite his aesthetic and axiological rebellion against the Palmah Generation, they reflect the same gender-determined dichotomies that inspired the fiction of his predecessors.

Unlike Pinhas Sadeh, who retained the heroic model in his androcentric fiction, many of the New Wave authors (including several Palmah authors) began to shift in the late 1950s to the anti-heroic model. This model tends to focus on disoriented male *schlemiel* who pursues false goals through a series of repeated defeats. In this context, the role of the male-authored female character is to embody these goals. Thus, for example, David Shahar's nameless protagonist in *The Moon of Honey and Gold* (1959) is inspired by his passion for Katherine to commit petty crimes and to compromise his integrity. Katherine, however, is a worthless, whorish servant maid who works for the protagonis't tight-fisted aunt, Stella. The protagonist recognizes Katherine's worthlessness only after he loses her to a rich German businessman. But if Katherine serves as the catalyst for the protagonist's misguided actions, it is never clear what motivates her. Why is she willing to sell her body to the highest bidder? Why does she betray her mistress in exchange for an expensive ring? Katherine's materialism is a given. It is never explained why the adulterous French *shiksa*, Sarah-Annette Martinez de Baillon, who thinks of all married women (herself included) as whores, indulges herself in a mindless affair with the protagonist.

One might argue that the motivations of Katherine and Sarah are irrelevant to the story, which is an allegorical critique of Israeli society. Katherine and Sarah are symbolizations of the materialistic and hedonistic ethos of capitalism. Yet this argument begs the question. For I seek to probe the conventional association of femininity with materialism. My question is, why do male Israeli authors tend to gynomorphize the goals or tendencies they criticize in their fiction?

Narcissism and materialism are the major motifs in the gyniconology of Lenny in Israel Eliraz's *A Summer of Gold* (1967). In contrast to the self-indulgent Lenny, who seems to be exclusively preoccupied by her appearance and who shows no concern for her dying mother, Amnon, her brother, it beset by tormenting thoughts about the personal and existential implications of his mother's impending death. Dinah Dolev's insatiable greed and sexual appetite in Yitzhak Shalev's *Blood and Spirit*

[1970] are also presented as intrinsic givens, highlighted by contrast the moral integrity of Daniel Dolev, her husband. Dinah's vacuous pursuit of consumer goods contrasts sharply with Daniel's preference for a modest lifestyle. As with so many other New Wave female characters, Dinah's materialism appears to be symptomatic of her unbridled sexuality. Her sexual excesses lead her to initiate an adulterous affair, while her husband seeks spiritual enlightenment. The hierarchical symbolizations of masculinity as spirit and femininity as matter also appear in Shamai Golan's *The Death of Uri Peled* (1971). Osnat Barzilai, the egotistical wife of Uri Peled, pressures him into leaving the army and taking up a respectable and lucrative job to satisfy her bourgeois needs. For the high-minded Uri Peled, a bourgeois career signifies an inescapable trap, which he finally flees through suicide. In essence, Osnat Barzilai is just as corrupt as her alter ego, the adulterous Mrs. Atzmon, who fornicates with army officers while her husband is fighting for national survival.

Materialism often combines with sexual perversion in contemporary male-created gyniconologies. As noted earlier, while male characters tend to approach sex instrumentally, either as a means to higher ends (Pinhas' in *Life as a Parable)*, or as an escape from an oppressive marriage (Adam in A.B. Yehoshua's *The Lover* 1977), or from existential ennui (Jacob in Jacob Buchan's *Jacob's Life*, 1979; Lazar in Jacob Shabtai's *Past Continuous*, 1977), female characters seem to consider sex an end in itself. Their sexuality appears to epitomize their very essence. Single women engage in sexual affairs, because they have nothing better to do. Examples are Yitzhak Orpaz's Batya in "Lyssanda's Death" 1964, Amos Oz's Noga Harish in *Elsewhere Perhaps* (1966), Shosh and Losh in Yehuda Amichai's *Hotel in the Wilderness* (1971), Zossi and Regina in Aharon Appelfeld's "Burning Light" (1980), and Jogette in David Schüt's "Abraham Rim" (1980). Similarly, married women commit adultery because they are by nature licentious and treacherous, like Mrs. Atzmon in Shamai Golan's *The Death of Uri Peled*, Ruth Kipnis in Amos Oz's "The Hill of Evil Counsel" (1976), Yutta in Yitzhak Ben Ner's "Rustic Sunset" (1976), and Dina in his "A Distant Land" (1981), and David Schütz's Lotta-Miriam in *The Grass and the Sand* (1978). Unlike the sexual affairs of men, which often serve as expressions of a deeper searching for meaning and identity, these hetaerae's pursuits only expose their inherent corruption.

While woman's materialism and sexuality manifest her moral and social Otherness, the frequent representations of woman as mad reflect her psychological Otherness. Male characters tend to *become* compulsive (for example, Max in Aharon Appelfeld's "Smoke," 1962) or psychotic (for example, Daniel in Yitzhak Orpaz's *Daniel's Voyage*, 1969) in response to *external* (social, political, or personal) factors, but female

characters seem to be *inherently*, inescapably, mad. Their actions and circumstances do not cause their temporary or permanent withdrawal
from reality, but rather gradually expose their sick souls. Thus, while
there is something noble, heroic, tragic, or even pathetic about the occa-
sional madness of male characters, female madness has no redeeming
features at all. While there is something inspiring in the aberrations of
Marian and Alyosha, the failed prophets and artists in Sadeh's *Life as a
Parable*, Adah and Havah, the nymphomaniacs, and especially Sarah, the
paranoid psychotic, are presented as clinically sick. Similarly, while the
mental breakdown of Yoel, the protagonist of Yehuda Amichai's *Not of
this Time not of This Place* (1963), is meticulously motivated and consequently moving and significant, his friend Minah's schizophrenia seems
to be inherent. Bertha, in Aharon Appelfeld's "Bertha" (1962) and Tzili in
"The Shirt and the Stripes" (1983) are both chronically retarded, and
because they were born with this mental disease, they are doomed to
live and die without the psychological breakthrough which often
redeems their male counterparts. Amos Oz's Hana Gonen in *My Michael*
(1968) grows into a full-fledged sadomasochist just as inevitably as Rim-
mona in his *Perfect Peace* (1982) is slow-witted. The schizophrenic klep-
tomaniac, Naomi, in A.B. Yehoshua's *Late Divorce* (1982) is just as in-
alterably schizophrenic as Vaducha in *The Lover* is anile. Many female
characters appear to regress into childhood as they grow older. Regres-
sion appears to be the lot of Yitzhak Ben Ner's Yutta in "Rustic Sunset"
(1976) and of the eponymous heroine of "Athalia" (1977). Just as there is
an innate inevitability about its inception, so is there something inex-
orable about the destructive consequences of female madness.

The moral and psychological Otherness of the female character in
the Generation of Statehood often intersects with what I will call, for
lack of a better term, "national Otherness." Whereas Palmah
gyniconologies sometimes typecast female foils as Jewish immigrants
(for example, Mika in Moshe Shamir's *He Went Through the Fields*), their
counterparts in the Generation of Statehood often emerge as non-Jewish
foreign women. Yet the function of the female outsider is essentially
similar in both generations. For while the femininity of the Jewish immigrant offers a bipolar corollary to the virile Sabra, the foreign woman
throws into relief the Jewish and Israeli identity of the male hero. The
symbolic aspect of the foreign woman who distracts the Israeli male
from his national duties suggests the threat that other countries, mainly
prosperous Western countries, pose to the ideals of socialist Zionism, or
the male national Self.[7]

To the extent that male-authored fiction of the Generation of
Statehood can be understood as an allegorical critique of the capitaliza-

tion and Westernization of Israeli society, its gyniconologies may be interpreted as embodiments of national Otherness, or of the false ideals that infiltrated the body politic from the West. The fact that male-created female foreigners are highly stereotyped—their major properties being foreignness (that is detachment from what preoccupies the male hero), materialism and hedonism—lends validity to the attempt to highlight their symbolic rather than their denotational or connotational function. But why is there such a high correlation between femininity and foreignness in male-authored contemporary fiction? Furthermore, what does this correlation mean in connotational terms—that is, what can it teach us about the cultural interpretation of womanhood in Israeli belles-lettres? May we interpret the gynomorphization of national Otherness as yet another manifestation of androcentric paranoia?

In A.B. Yehoshua's *Early in the Summer of 1970* (1972), the protagonist's American daughter-in-law is disarmingly naive to the sociopolitical context of Israel during the war of attrition, even when her own husband is drafted and mistakenly reported killed in action. In dramatic contrast to her married lover Yehuda, the American Connie in Yehoshua's *Late Divorce* (1982) seems equally detached from the Israeli context, even after her immigration from America. The American Patricia in Yehuda Amichai's *Not of this Time not of this Place* (1959) is just as seductive and detached from the national context as are her counterparts in Yehoshua's fiction. There is, in fact, a direct correlation between her sexual desirability and her foreignness, for Patricia offers Joel, the protagonist, an escape not only from his constricting marriage to the Israeli Mira, but also from Israeli reality in general. This sexy *shiksa* offers the male hero a delightful escape from marital and national responsibility, as do the French Sarah-Annette Martinez de Baillon in David Shahar's *The Moon of Honey and Gold*, Orlan's Scandinavian beauty in Moshe Shamir's *The Border* (1966), the Spanish Nora in Benjamin Tammuz's *At the Edge of the West* (1966), the Polish Yutta in Yitzhak Ben Ner's "Rustic Sunset," and the German Inga in Aharon Megged's *Voyage in Ab* (1980). The hero's flight from Israeli reality into the arms of a foreign belle is usually short-lived. The native Israeli hero—be it Joel, Orlan, Elik, or Gidi—is either incapable of evading his national duty for good or unwilling to do so. In most male-authored mythogynies, the foreign woman is abandoned when the male hero comes to his senses. Few of the narratives permit the foreign woman entry into the national context. Her detachment from that context is just as inevitable as the male hero's reawakening to his responsibilities and the implications of his national identity.

To the extent that they are indifferent to the nation's predicaments and wish to leave the country—that is, betray in the deepest way the Zionist ideal—even native Israeli women emerge from male-authored works as foreign. A.B. Yehoshua's sleepy wife in *Missile Base 612* (1975) is just as indifferent to the national context as is the slow-witted Yael in *Late Divorce.* After many years in Israel, the psychotic Mrs. Goldman in Jacob Shabtai's *Past Continuous* (1977) pretends she is back in her native country Poland. Poland is also the beloved homeland of the mentally disturbed Yutta in Yitzhak Ben Ner's "Rustic Sunset." Hana in Amos Oz's *My Michael* dreams about the snow-covered German city of Danzig. Despite years of living in their real Jewish homeland, women—immigrants and natives—have no qualms about betraying Zionism by leaving for the very countries which threatened to annihilate the Jewish people. What typifies these women is their apparent lack of hesitation or regret. Ideals or ennobling principles never interfere with their questionable motives. Driven by materialism, Eva Harish in Oz's *Elsewhere Perhaps* (1966) leaves her kibbutz for Germany, while Aya in Aharon Megged's *Asahel* (1978)—abdicates Israel in pursuit of her Palestinian lover.

One must keep in mind that the word for 'emigration' in Hebrew [yerida] means 'descending' and carries pejorative connotations. Moreover, as Robert Alter notes, extending the horizons of the literary work into foreign landscapes is not only a means of dealing with a sense of national claustrophobia in a small country hemmed in by a hostile environment but "the figure of the expatriate is used to put to the test some of the fundamental assumptions of the Israeli national enterprise."[8] It is therefore significant that female expatriates appear to have no conflicts or misgivings about their emigration, while their male counterparts—from Moshe Wolf in Hanoch Bartov's *The Account and the Spirit* (1953) to Ami in Yoram Kaniuk's *Rockinghorse* (1973) and Gershon Rieger in Aharon Megged's *The Bat* (1975)—are obsessed with guilt and fond memories of their homeland. And while none of the male-authored female expatriates returns to her homeland, her male counterparts often do, even if they do it halfheartedly.

The failure of the Generation of Statehood to challenge the Palmah Generation's stereotyping of woman as Other may be explained in terms of its authors susceptibility to symbolic expression and social critique. As noted earlier, the new gynomorphization of the corrupt society replaced the Palmah Generation's gynomorphization of the private sphere. In symbolic terms, the mad, materialistic, hedonistic, and adulterous wife symbolizes the most objectionable aspects of an emerging bourgeois, urban, competitive society. In male-authored allegorical critiques, the mad wife stands for Israel's ideological disorientation, while her materialism embodies the increasing consumerism of a capitalistic economy. Similarly, her adultery may symbolize Israel's betrayal of the original socialist Zionist values, while her foreignness underscores the suspicious source of the false values so many of the new authors decry. As noted earlier, the war between the sexes often serves as a parabolic representation of the set of conflicts which emerged between nation and land, and between ideology and society. The breakup of families and marriages has become a common metaphor for the much-lamented transition of Israel from a community of dedicated volunteers and visionaries to a Westernized state embroiled in war and stultified by narrow pragmatism and partisan politics.

Within this symbolic economy, there is an unmistakable hierarchy of male and female roles. Works like A.B. Yehoshua's *Late Divorce*, which tend to use the husband as the symbol of the disoriented nation, gynomorphize the land. The once-beloved wife turned old, undersirable, and dangerous is an eloquent symbol for a once-beloved homeland turned trap. The gynomorphic representation of the country draws not only on the fact that all terms for 'country' (eretz), 'land' (adama), 'state' (medina), or 'motherland' (moledet) are of the female gender, but also on an established literary tradition with roots in the Hebrew Bible. But while in medieval poetry the land of Israel is portrayed as a deserted widow and in modern Palestinian fiction as a beautiful bride (or patient mother) awaiting the return of her lover (or son), in current Israeli literature, for somewhat obvious reasons, the land is often symbolized by a treacherous mother or wife, hungry for ever-greater male sacrifices.

For the male national Self, escaping from the land is a foredoomed effort. A.B. Yehoshua's Yehuda in *Late Divorce* makes an attempt to divorce his wife after a prolonged stay in the United States, where he has established a new relationship with the younger more seductive Connie [the new "land"]. But shortly after securing his divorce, on his way to the United States, Yehuda stops by his wife's asylum, where he is clobbered to death by one of the asylum's inmates. Like Yehuda, Jacob in Yitzhak Orpaz's *Ants* (1968) seems helpless in his relations with his beautiful, mad, frigid, sadistic wife Rachel. Critics have been quick to note that Rachel symbolizes the beloved and cruel land of Israel, whose possession entails endless suffering on the part of the nation. On the other hand, Rachel, who engorges herself on honey and thereby attracts hordes of monstrous ants to the house (often referred to as *"hablaniot"* the Hebrew designation for 'terrorists'), may be interpreted as the self-destructive

drive in a nation gone awry.[9] But whatever symbolic interpretation we
prefer, the fact remains that Rachel is the real cause of the destruction
of the house.

The point I am making is that even when we accept the critical
tendency to interpret contemporary Israeli fiction as allegorical
representations of the national predicament, we must not ignore the
problematic association of femininity with what is presented in the particular work as the source of social and national trouble. Even if I were
to focus primarily on the allegorical interpretation—which I do not—I
still find in the symbolic level the misogynous premises which underlie
the denotational and connotational levels of Israeli male-created
gyniconologies. The problem of the sexual hierarchy does not disappear
when we assign symbolic functions to male and female characters. The
fact is that having been expanded into symbolic and national realms,
male-authored gyniconologies have become even more problematical.
For, as we have seen, the general tendency is to cast the female
character in the role of a social and national Other, as that mysterious
force that risks undermining the entire national enterprise. In what
follows, I shall take a closer look at the strategies and possible implications of the male tendency to present women not only as the enemies of
individual men, but as the enemies of the entire nation.

The Female Other as National Enemy

In an essay on the new Israeli story, Baruch Kurzweil argues that
since the early 1960s, Israeli fiction has demonstrated an increasing
obsession with the subject of Eros. Kurzweil refers to Eros not in its
Freudian sense of the 'life instinct,' but in the sense of "the temptations
of woman," and as such he uses it as a term of opprobrium: "But this
special conspicuousness of Eros, which is so characteristic of so many
Israeli stories, testifies to the lack of a real goal in life. This mania for
Eros in the Hebrew story is not a sign of effervescent vitality, but of
something sick. It signifies the escape from the emptiness of life."[10] Kurzweil goes on to interpret the proliferation of stories about the sexual
"temptations of woman" not only as a manifestation of existential ennui
but also as an expression of national self-hatred, an attempt to flee from
Jewish identity to a suicidal pursuit of false Western idols. Although
Kurzweil rightly calls attention to the thematic ascendancy of what he
calls Eros, he ignores the fact that Eros (in Kurzweil's sense) is con-
sistently linked to Thanatos, the death instinct. The reason that Eros "is
not a sign of effervescent vitality, but of something sick" is that

heterosexual love in the literature of the New Wave is *presented* as a sick and suicidal pursuit. Instead of examining the fictional representation of heterosexual love and national war, instead of questioning the gynomorphization of death, Kurzweil appears to endorse the idea that "the temptations of woman" are by definition deadly. In what follows, I would like to both problematize and offer some explanations for the frequent association of death and femininity in male-authored, war-related stories of the 1960s and 1970s.

The thematic combination of heterosexual love and war is not unique to the Generation of Statehood. It appears with great frequency in works by S. Yizhar, Moshe Shamir, and Nathan Shaham, to name only a few of the leading authors of what is known as the Palmah Generation (1948–1958). Almost all war-related stories of the Palmah Generation contain one or more subplots revolving around heterosexual love. What characterizes these works, however, is the contrast between love and war. In the works of S. Yizhar, the image of a beloved woman glows in the imagination of the male fighter as an incandescent source of hope, a symbol of peace and life. From his early short stories to his novel, *The Days of Ziklag* (1958), Yizhar portrays his women as symbols of love over against his beleaguered male fighters. Moshe Shamir does not share Yizhar's tendency to idealize his female characters, but he too tends to contrast heterosexual love with the sacrifices of war. In *He Went Through the Fields* (1948), Uri's love affair with Mika contrasts with his death during a military training session. His world of war and struggle is discontinuous with her world of love and romance. Thus in the Palmah fiction, war and heterosexual love emerge as opposite thematic poles, represented respectively by the male protagonist and his perennial lover.

By contrast, the Generation of Statehood presents love as an extension of war. Heterosexual love becomes an ugly and destructive power struggle that leads to atrophy and death. The female character, previously symbolic of peacefulness and security, turns into a pernicious predator. Romantic love, which is often idealized in the Palmah Generation as the loftiest human drive, is portrayed as mechanical sex, degrading and debilitating for both the man and the woman involved. Love and war parallel and complement rather than oppose each other.

This gyniconological transformation is adumbrated in Yoram Kaniuk's *Himo: King of Jerusalem* (1966). The novel revolves around the peculiar love of the young and beautiful nurse Hamutal Hurvitz for Himo, a casualty of the 1948 War of Independence. The only unmutilated remainder of what used to be a dashing young officer are Himo's lips, which convulsively and incessantly mumble, "Shoot me!"

"Shoot me!" The rest of his body, including, most significantly, his genitals, is irreparably damaged. Undeterred by Himo's ghastly physique, Hamutal showers all her love and devotion on him, to the astonishment and envy of the other wounded soldiers in the hospital. Finally, however, Hamutal gives up and decides to poison Himo to put an end to his agony. But just as Hamutal is preparing the fatal injection, Himo undergoes a strange transformation. He is shown to suddenly recover his long-extinct desire to live: "He was pleading for his life. His mutilated body was writhing now. He tried to stretch out his hands imploringly. He pleaded like a starving dog, but he could no more say a word."[11]

The juxtaposition of the upright stature of the beautiful nurse boldly gripping the poisonous injector and the prone male patient writhing helplessly at her feet may be read as symptomatic of a male paranoid response to the reversal of sexual power relations occasioned by war. I would like to suggest that the transformation of Hamutal from an icon of love to an angel of death reveals an androcentric myth presenting wars as experiences which are likely to emasculate the "strong sex" and to empower the "weak sex" male victims at the mercy of female nurses, and male survivors depend on female services and nurturance.[12]

By presenting, at the end of the story, a calm and collected Hamutal stopping at a coffee shop several years later and remembering the tragic incident only in passing, Kaniuk's novel subverts the romantic image of woman in the Palmah literature as protective mother or lover as well as that of the perennial mourner. It is true that Hamutal's love for Himo supplies the motivation for the larger part of the novel, but the ironic denouement challenges the impression previously created. Hamutal's decision to kill Himo turns out to be just as irrational and unpredictable as her unyielding love for him. Both are incongruous with the desires and needs of the male victim. Woman's proverbial selflessness is here exposed as irrational and transient. Even woman's deepest identifications with the male victim, even the most passionate love, is shown to have its limit. At best, woman is an outsider in war; at worst, she is a dangerous enemy in the guise of a caring, nurturing healer.

In Amos Oz's novel *My Michael* (1968), the symbolic representation of woman as Thanatos in the guise of Eros becomes even more explicit. Although this novel also presents the man, Michael, as victim and the woman, Hana, as victimizer, the novel celebrates the male victim's quiet victory over his destructive enemy. For despite Hana's refusal to cooperate with Michael, either as wife or as mother, it is she who finally degenerates through successive stages of boredom, passivity, and physical sickness into psychosis, while Michael succeeds in launching a brilliant academic career, moving progressively towards greater professional accomplishments and economic stability. Hana's perverse attitude to her husband is more eloquently presented in her sexual exploitation of his body: "I would wake up my husband, crawl under his blanket, cling to his body with all my might . . . Nevertheless, I ignored him; I made contact only with his body: muscles, arms, hair. In my heart I knew that I betrayed him over and over again with his body."[13] Using Michael as a sex object, Hana turns what constitutes the ultimate symbolic expression of love into a ritualistic enactment of war. Having failed to vitiate her husband's virility by other means, she attempts to castrate him by exhausting him sexually. Hana is incapable of love and uninterested in it. What she seeks is sadomasochistic titillation, a luxury her dedicated husband does not afford her. She therefore resorts to erotic fantasies in which she is both the commander and the victim of Halil and Aziz, her Palestinian childhood playmates, whom she imagines to have become terrorists. It is significant that Hana first starts to fantasize about Halil and Aziz when Michael is drafted during the war of 1954. The analogy between the husband who is fighting the Egyptians in the Sinai peninsula and the wife who indulges in erotic fantasies about Palestinian terrorists dramatizes Hana's conjugal *and* national disloyalty. Her growing distance from Michael parallels her growing hostility against the state. At the end of the novel, Hana imagines herself sending her Palestinian lovers and servants on an anti-Israeli terrorist mission. By evening both will crouch to prepare their supplies for the journey. "I will set them on . . . faded military backpacks, a box of explosives, detonators, fuses, ammunition, handgranades, glittering knives."[14]

The frequent presentation of wives as conjugal and national enemies reveals, among other things, a deep-seated suspicion of women's allegedly passive role in wartime. The notion that married women stay home, secure and relatively invulnerable, while men sacrifice their lives to defend them has powerful implications for intersexual relations in a country like Israel, which is constantly threatened by war. It must be remembered that despite the compulsory draft in Israel, only 50 percent of draftable women actually join the armed forces. Religious, illiterate, married, and pregnant women are exempted from the draft.[15] Furthermore, the law debars women from combat duties; consequently, the majority of women serve in auxiliary jobs (as, for example, secretaries, clerks, teachers, drivers, wireless operators, and parachute folders). These circumstances create the impression that women are not really involved in the war effort, that their suffering and sacrifices are negligible compared to the price exacted from the male fighters. This impression reinforces the entrenched stereotype of the dynamic male and the passive female.

In the volatile political context of Israel, a country continuously on the brink of military conflagration, passivity may be feared as treachery, or worse, as a perverse subconscious attraction to the national enemy. Fostered, on the one hand, by the archetypal association of treachery with female sexuality, and by the popularization of the Freudian theory of female masochism on the other hand, this vision spawns an image very much like that of Hana Gonen, a woman who indulges in orgiastic fantasies of rape by Palestinian terrorists while her husband fights for the survival of Israel.[16]

If the implicitly incriminating portrait of Hana Gonen derives from the subconscious mistrust of the homebound passive woman, Yitzhak Ben Ner's "Nicole" (1976) is inspired by the apparently opposite distrust of the active army woman. While Hana's passivity and unsociability are unacceptable by the standards of socialist Zionism, Nicole's participation in the army is threatening the traditional Judeo-Christian endorsement of woman's place in the home. Like Hamutal and Hana, Nicole is beautiful and sexy; like Hana, Nicole wields her sexuality as a weapon in her eternal contest with men she wants to subdue. Unlike Hana, however, Nicole is not content with fantasies of self-destruction. To satisfy her sadomasochistic proclivities, she joins the army and ends by destroying others. What attracts Nicole to a career in the army is not patriotism or even a professional interest, but the vulnerability of the sex-starved soldiers—the perfect potential victims for her narcissism and nymphomania. The story focuses on Nicole's sexual campaigns and conquests, especially on her affair with Lieutenant Colonel Baruch Adar, or Barko, whom she seduces away from his lawful wife, as she has done with all her previous lovers. On the eve of the fearful Yom Kippur of 1973, she convinces Barko to spend the night with her in a hotel whose location remains undisclosed to their brigade. When the war breaks out, the soldiers cannot contact Lieutenant Barko, and the result is confusion, disorientation, and ultimately defeat. Although Barko blames himself for the defeat of his brigade, there is sufficient evidence to suggest that the real cause of the defeat is Nicole. The aetiological link of one of the most traumatic wars in Israel's history with the wiles and guiles of a military woman reveals a deep-seated distrust of women soldiers, especially of those endowed with authoritative status. When allowed to affect the public scene, woman evolves from a personal to a national enemy; her vampire bite affects not only the individual man, but the entire army.

But in addition to the distrust of women in power, women who endanger the traditional power-structured status quo between the sexes, the story reveals a deeper discontent with women's encroachment into what has long been an exclusively male domain. The next monologue, in which Amiram castigates Nicole for her irresponsibility, reveals not only contempt for military women in power, but a vision of woman as an outsider who is incapable of comprehending even the most basic facts about the army: "Look madame, this is the army. This is an army at war for life or death. In such a war, things must be decided like that, sharply this or that way. You have been among us long enough to understand this, haven't you?"[17] Amiram implies that, despite Nicole's status and experience, she has remained a woman, an outsider, over against "us," the male insiders. Amiram's condescension can be understood as a protest against Nicole's intrusion into a traditionally male sphere of activity. Successful military women may compromise the traditional image of male fighters and defenders of women and children and may also undermine the ethos of male bonding. Symbolically identified with sex and sensuality, women threaten the military ethos, which thrives on the cultivation of toughness and the suppression of Eros. In a military context, woman is reduced to a sex object and sex to a mechanical activity intended to relieve physiological tensions rather than to gratify emotional needs. Because one must not give in to normal human needs for love and intimacy, women and sex become objects of derision.[18]

Like Hamutal Hurvitz and Hana Gonen, Nicole is the epitome of the castrating bitch, who, under the guise of love, emasculates her male victims: "She is so glad to know that he [Barko] is afraid. At last. He should be afraid. She wants him to be afraid."[19] Like Hana Gonen, Nicole sadistically tortures her man in an attempt to destroy his virility and to subject him to her will. Realizing how guilty Barko feels about the brigade's defeat, she calls him up, pretending to be a widow of one of his dead soldiers. But in the battle between the sexes, Nicole, like Hana, cannot win. With resentment and exasperation, Nicole admits her defeat: "But, damn it, he does not crawl, break down, quiver, cry, scream, writhe helplessly. He always rises after he falls."[20] Once again, a man is victimized not by national but by sexual war; the real enemy is not the Arab across the border, but the Israeli woman inside the hospital, the home, or the camp. The most fatal blows come not from firearms, but from the loving arms of women. Death lurks not in violence, but in sexuality.

It seems to me that the gynomorphization of military defeat in the Generation of Statehood is the product of both political and literary factors. Israel's protracted war with the Arabs, a war whose inevitability and complexity began to emerge in Israel's cultural consciousness after the war of 1956, has created what Marcuse calls "a repressive society," a society in which death is feared as a constant threat, glorified as a supreme sacrifice, or accepted as an inescapable fate.[21] In a repressive culture, Eros is feared as a distracting, energy-consuming principle. Instead of allowing human sexuality to sublimate itself into Eros—a life-giving social order—a repressive system suppresses it by trivializing it, reducing it to a biological need and presenting it as potentially dangerous. On a less abstract level, Israel's protracted war, combined with the sexual division of labor within the army, produces a suspicion of women who seem to not quite do their share, despite their traditional nurturing and protective roles as wives and mothers outside the army or as nurses and auxiliary soldiers within the army. On the other hand, the constant threat of war and the continuous political instability create a strong need for security within the private sphere, a need which is often translated into a nostalgic vision of the patriarchal tradition. Consequently, untraditional powerful women, especially women of authority in the army, are likely to inspire distrust and anxiety.

The conflict between the Jewish traditional definition of womanhood and the secular Zionist one can be traced in a keynote speech about the status of women in the army delivered by David Ben Gurion to the first Knesset. The tension between the biblical expectation that the woman of valor be first and foremost a good mother and the modern expectation that she be a loyal citizen with public responsibilities is reinscribed rather than resolved in Ben Gurion's historic speech. The implied addressees of this speech appear to be the members of the religious parties who opposed the draft of women, and one could argue that the concessive conclusion according to which women will only receive basic training and not be allowed into combat must be understood within the framework of party politics. Yet another less obvious group of addressees are the women who participated in military combat in the prestate era and who have grown out of the notion that their mission in life is to bear children.

> Now, for the question of women in the army. When one discusses the position of women, two factors must be taken into consideration. First, women have a special mission as mothers. There is no greater mission in life, and nature has decreed that only a woman can give birth to a child. This is a woman's task and her blessing. However, a second factor must be remembered; the woman is not only a woman, but a personality in her own right in the same way as a man. As such, she should enjoy the same rights and responsibilities as the man, except where motherhood is concerned. There are members of this House who feel differently. That is their privilege, but the majority of the community accepts the basic principle that women cannot be allowed to occupy a lower position in society than men."[22]

The co-optation of the religious subtext by the secularist text is made possible through a naturalistic interpretation of religious doctrine. Since God can no longer be invoked as a source of authority, the secular text invokes nature as the authoritative force which has alleged power to "decree" or valorize women's "special mission as mothers." There is, however, an inconsistency in the simultaneous presentation of woman's procreative role as both natural and vocational, or "decreed." If motherhood is natural, why recommend it as a noble "mission"—a word which implies a voluntary decision and has unmistakably religious [though not necessarily Jewish traditional] connotations? As noted earlier, part of the answer lies in the attempt to convince those women who have rejected their traditional "mission" to embrace it again. Thus while the secular text affirms the "basic principle that women cannot be allowed to occupy a lower position in society than men," it nevertheless replicates the basic principle of the traditional sexually segregated community which assigns different roles and responsibilities to men and women. By stressing woman's procreative role, the would-be egalitarian text reinscribes—through commendation rather than legal decree—the traditional perception of woman as mother and wife.

The monstrous gyniconologies we find in male-created war stories reinscribe in a slightly different way the syncretic mythogyny underlying Ben Gurion's text. The expectation that woman should nurture "like a woman" and fight "like a man" explains the lurid androgyny of fictional women like Hana Gonen, Nicole, and, to a lesser extent, Hamutal Hurvitz. In an embattled country like Israel, the implications of a group's lesser involvement in the military effort may easily be interpreted as sinister, if not outright hostile. What is rarely remembered is that male-authored texts, whether legal or fictional, are creating the objectionable conditions they are condemning as the results of women's wiles.

It is possible to argue with Sandra Gilbert that the vindictive male-created gyniconologies in the Generation of Statehood are symptoms of phallic anxiety: the punitive treatment by male authors of the army nurse or woman soldier expresses a threatened virility traditionally symbolized by martial prowess and male bonding. Gilbert suggests that "as young men became alienated from their prewar selves, increasingly immured in the muck and blood of No Man's Land, women seemed to become, as if by some uncanny swing of history's pendulum, ever more powerful."[23] On the other hand, the inferior status of Israeli women authors suggests that the allegedly salutary relationship of women and war described by Gilbert is not a universal paradigm. The small number of Israeli women authors who have been admitted to the canon and the even smaller number of women authors who address Israel's war in their fiction suggest that, if anything, war has had as contrary an impact on them as it has had on male-created women. Israeli literary women seem to be anything but empowered by the protracted war with the Arabs. There is no trace of national-or gender-related victoriousness in the works of Netiva Ben-Yehuda, herself a Palmah commander and one of the few women who address the subject in writing. It took Ben Yehuda over three decades to commit to paper her thoughts and feelings about the War of Independence. But instead of a sense of power or pride, we find in *1984—Between the Calendars* (1981) and *Through the Binding Ropes* (1985) a satiric and disillusioned view of the excesses of young men and women who found themselves embroiled in a historic war for national independence. The Israeli case does not bear out the idea that war is an empowering experience for literary women.

Most of the fiction produced by the Generation of Statehood in the 1960s and 1970s, however, represents war as the exclusive preserves of men, in terms of both heroic struggle and the victimization involved. As already noted, what is even more striking is the punitive gyniconologies created by male authors. A helpful insight into the possible relationship between Israel's worsening mythogynies and its protracted state of war is offered by Peggy Reeves Sanday's study of the impact of stress on the status of women in different societies. According to Reeves Sanday, the condemnation of women is a common response to stress: "When people sense that their universe is out of order, that they are victims of circumstances beyond their control, they look among themselves for the oppressor, or they examine their behavior for wrongdoing, or they do both . . . People respond to the disorder by fixing blame and establishing punishments in order to restore balance. Who or what is blamed and how and why affects the relationship between the sexes."[24]

The prevailing sense in Israeli narratives of the 1960s and 1970s is that the world indeed is out of kilter. More often than not, male-female relationships are used to symbolize the war, or, vice versa, war is used to symbolize the topsy-turvy relationship. The implicitly punitive gyniconologies in Israeli, war-related narratives is related to the human need to blame the troubles of the group on insiders. The symbolic affixation of blame on women is an expression of self-blame, but the Self that is being blamed is that part of it which is Other. Woman is more stereotyped and condemned than characters of Arabs, for example, which on the whole are sympathetically protrayed because they seem not to share the national identity of the group. To use René Girard's theory of ritual sacrifice, woman's liminal status as both a national insider and a national outsider makes her a better symbolic victim. Girard explains that in successful sacrificial ritual, the victim destined to symbolically absorb the violence of the group must both share the group's identity and remain outside it.[25] The Israeli woman is most appropriate as a symbolic sacrificial victim because, unlike the Arab, she shares the Israeli identity as defined by national ethos. But while she shares the important aspects of the national Self, she is different; her sexuality defines her as an outsider. Thus, mythical reasoning targets woman as the nation's real enemy.

But comtemporary Israeli literature reflects not only the effects of war and siege. To a large extent, it is also what Yosef Oren calls "a literature of disillusionment."[26] The gradual transformation of a pioneer, idealistic society into an embattled, highly bureaucratized state often takes the shape, in Israeli fiction, of a woman who has gone mad. The internecine relations between husband and wife and the degeneration of love into mutually destructive sex serve as metaphors for what Israeli writers perceive as Israel's ideological and social disintegration. These metaphors often function as rhetorical warnings. As Yosef Oren points out: "The writers of the new generation dramatize an extreme scene, that has not yet been concretized in Israeli reality, and ask us to accept it as an authentic testimony of the reality of our lives."[27] Identified with the family, the fundamental unit of society, women have come to signify the stultifying, hypocritical and corrupt society from which the Israeli male hero constantly flees, often right into the arms of war. Thus the romanticized, nurturing mother and lover of the Palmah generation—often the symbol of civilian life—has become the castrating lover in the literature of the 1960s and 1970s. To the extent that private relations serve as national symbols, the vampire woman reflects not only the exasperating society, but also the devouring country, insatiably hungry for male victims. The land of Israel is often symbolically portrayed as a female principle, a conception with deep biblical roots. But whereas in utopian literature of the 1920–30s it appeared as a loving mother and wife, it emerges in Hebrew fiction of the 1960s and 70s as a kind of *femme fatale*, at once desirable and dangerous for her male lovers.

Baruch Kurzweil was right in observing the increasing prevalence of what he calls "Eros" in Israeli literature, but his interpretation of this development can only be accepted if we consider its full range. It is not merely the increasing preponderance of women that conveys a sense of disorientation and existential ennui. It is rather the presentation of women as symbols of death that may perhaps signal an expression of despair in Israeli fiction. It is the pervasive combination of Eros with Thanatos that may convey what Kurzweil sees as the flight from affirming values to self-hatred and self-destruction.

CHAPTER 3

A.B. Yehoshua: The Lack of Consciousness

From his early phantasmatic parables staged against a barely identifiable background of time and place to his later more realistic novels, Yehoshua's fictions have tended to focus on the misadventures of endearingly wayward eccentrics.[1] Frequently the defeated anti-heroes of romantic or domestic dramas, Yehoshua's comic, pathetic protagonists fail both in obtaining a desirable woman and in breaking away from undesirable wives. Rarely aware of their real needs, they are busy pursuing questionable solutions which further trammel them in interlocking chains of increasingly absurd events and exacerbate their initial problems. As with most comic characters, they rarely reach the stage of self-awareness necessary for genuine development.[2] Their senseless quests often propel them towards a climactic self-defeat which exposes rather than transforms their vulnerabilities and the hopelessness of their situation.

To the extent that these scenarios can be read as parables of national malaise alluding, for example, to the nation's ideological disorientation or to its suicidal involvement in endless wars, Yehoshua continues the Palmah's tradition of combining narrative art and social critique. Yet this very continuity reveals the important ways in which Yehoshua has departed from both the poetic and ideological orientation of his predecessors.[3] For unlike his predecessors, who used the sociopolitical condition of their time as their primary mimetic materials, Yehoshua apparently introduces mimetic materials as a mere background to his protagonists' familial and psychological dramas. Largely marginalized by most of the Palmah authors, the private sphere—featuring a panoply of neurotic individuals and torn-up families—becomes the mimetic focus of Yehoshua's fiction.

Although many critics have been too eager to allegorize Yehoshua's fiction, I tend to agree that his work can be read as a symbolic critique of Israeli society. In this context, we may be right in interpreting the frequent descriptions of failed marriages as images of the nation's malaise. In an essay about the relationship between Zionism and the Jewish Diaspora, Yehoshua explains the Diaspora as a neurotic symptom of a son who has been all too long separated from his mother [the land of Israel].[4]

The importance of the symbolic aspect of Yehoshua's fiction should not occlude, however, our interest in his mimetic materials, specifically in his gyniconologies and their relationship to his predecessors in the Palmah Generation. My argument is that, from a mythogynous point of view, Yehoshua did not break with the tradition of the Palmah. His female characters are both mimetically and structurally dependent for meaning on their male counterparts. Most of Yehoshua's female characters are passive, and most of them lack the consciousness necessary for experiencing the confusion which is the perennial state of his male characters. The itinerary of his female characters is determined by the absurd quests of his male heroes, who may be laughable but who are nevertheless aware that there is something askew in their lives.

The passivity of Yehoshua's female characters is closely related to their inability to think, as is the case in other male-authored gyniconologies.[5] One may speculate that the perennial blankness of Yehoshua's female characters is necessitated by their structural function as the foils of their male counterparts and the catalysts of their actions. It would surely be improper to endow the secondary characters with more interesting or significant capabilities than those enjoyed by the focal characters. And since the focal characters are rarely conscionable or heroic, only a combination of humorless blankness, a hopeless inscrutability, and a stereotypic simplicity should be able to highlight the redeeming features of their chronic deficiencies.[6]

Even in Yehoshua's later multifocal novels, female characters are relegated to an auxiliary status. Since, as in the Palmah Generation, they perform male-related roles (lovers, wives), their contribution to nondomestic or nonmarital dramas is slim. This fact explains the marginality of female characters in narratives focusing on such themes as the effects of a prolonged military conflict ("The Last Commander", "Opposite the Forests", "Missile Base 612") or the intricacies of intergenerational conflict ("A Poet's Prolonged Silence", "Early in the Summer of 1970"). Defined a priori as male domains, "universal" dramas about parents and children or war and peace rarely accommodate female characters even in their usual secondary status, relegating them instead to peripheral, almost expendable roles.

Whether Yehoshua's plots are used "to explore the shadowy under-side of ambivalence in an Israeli consciousness beleaguered by unrelen-ting conflict with the Arabs" or to illuminate the vacuity of modern ex-istence, they are contingent on male actions and experiences.[7] As the lovers and wives of Yehoshua's eccentric male characters, his female characters represent at best the walls against which the males beat their heads.[8] As human extensions of a world gone awry, they embody the causes of their male counterparts' malaise while apparently lacking the capacity to share it. Their blankness does not permit them to experience the loss, confusion, and panic driving their male counterparts. Their passivity denies them the redeeming aspects of the male characters' com-ically ineffective enterprises.

Another feature which generally separates Yehoshua's male and female characters is the female's association with the domestic sphere. It is not that his male characters are adequately aware of their social con-texts, but that they interact with society more frequently and mean-ingfully. This gender-determined distinction may owe its existence to what Elizabeth Janeway calls the "social mythology about women's natural preference for the domestic sphere."[9] Perhaps more important-ly, the implicit judgment of Yehoshua's female characters is directly related to their success as wives or mothers. The implicit judgment of Yehoshua's male characters, by contrast, is directly related to their social and political responsibilities.

To facilitate my discussion of Yehoshua's mythogynies, I have divid-ed his female characters into three major categories: the desirable but unattainable young woman, the inaccessible or undesirable wife, and the old woman. While the young woman emerges mostly as a sex object, the old woman is rarely associated with sex, while the mature woman, usual-ly a wife, is always problematic, either because she is excessively frigid or because she is oversexed. Despite these differences, all seem to share a peculiar sort of mental blankness which appears to become exacer-bated as their sexual potential diminishes. Thus, the older woman is like-ly to develop into a psychopath, while the young woman is simply mindless.

The greater visibility and apparent autonomy of female characters in Yehoshua's later words seem to corroborate his contention that female characters "scare" him "less and less."[10] Yet, as we shall see, the dif-ference between his later and earlier female characters is not substan-tial. Largely confined to male-related roles, Yehoshua's later female characters are products of an androcentric imagination, though their stereotyping is not as obvious.

Yehoshua's *Belle Dame Sans Merci*

Rarely capable of thinking or feeling, Yehoshua's early adolescent beauty exists primarily to be sexually captured by the male protagonist. Predictably, however, female beauty entails that its possessor be unattainable, and thus the hero's quest for his chimerical love inevitably leads to catastrophe. What is never too clear is to what extent Yehoshua's *belle dame sans merci* is aware of the protagonist's anguish.

That the unattainable beauty is best understood as a projection of male anxiety is best exemplified by one of Yehoshua's earliest stories, "The Day's Sleep," which is included in his first collection of stories, *The Death of the Old Man* (1963). Overcome by sudden exhaustion, the nameless narrator interrupts his work at a construction site and follows his workmate Lubrani to the latter's apartment, where he falls into a deep and long sleep. The climactic moment in the story is the narrator's oneiric encounter with an elusive image of a young, beautiful woman: "Naked and dark [she was] stretched out on the grass among the trees, along the contours of the tortuous wadi. I dived into her brown, dim eyes, seeking her body silently and passionately. She caressed my face, and I was overcome by pleasure. I threw myself upon her smooth body, burning in the desire of my kisses."[11]

After this euphoric encounter, however, the narrator soon finds himself sinking deeper into the river, until he almost drowns: "But I already began losing the woman; slipping and sinking to wallow in the river itself. My lips have lost the woman's sweet skin and began kissing the flowing water . . . . My entire body was swallowed in the wet earth, with only my head sticking above the ground" (p. 38). On the verge of drowning, the narrator wakes up. The point of complete separation from the phantom girl is also the point at which he returns to reality. To an extent, the seductive object of desire explains the protagonist's sudden exhaustion and may symbolize his desire for the land of Israel and the price of this desire. Gershon Shaked, for example, suggests that the motif of Thanatos running through *The Death of the Old Man* is suggestive of the suicidal pathos of a war-ravaged generation.[12]

Whether seen in a national or a universal context, the female image in this collection tends to appear in opposition to the images of productive labor and social responsibility. The female is often presented as the seductive object of desire which finally drains the male subject of energy and gradually lures him to self-destruction. Although the young beauties we shall discuss next emerge as "real" women rather than mere figments of a male's dream, they too embody the dangerous objects of a perverse suicidal desire, if not the seductive agents of death itself.

"Galia's Wedding," an eerie story about unrequited love and jealousy, features a gorgeous, blue-eyed, fair-haired Galia and five male victims: the protagonist-narrator, who pines away for her without ever divulging his secret; Ardon, Ido, and Itai, her former lovers; and Dani, her newly married husband. The four lovers are tortured by their unreciprocated love and obsession with Galia, and the much envied Dani falls prey to their jealous fury. Having boarded the same bus to kibbutz Sedot Yam, the four taunt and physically abuse the newly wedded husband.

While the four desperadoes are hopelessly obsessed with Galia, she is only vaguely aware of their existence. She appears to have rejected her lovers as casually as she ignores their violent assault on Dani. She responds to the narrator's passionate embrace as he takes his leave from her shortly after her wedding ceremony with the same arbitrariness: "She began collapsing in my arms. 'My brother, my brother.' Her voice was choking as her fingers ploughed through my hair." (A.D., p. 55). While Yehoshua makes some effort to explain the motivations of the male characters, he makes no effort to explain Galia. Lacking the jealousy which is driving her male counterparts, Galia is drifting through this hallucinatory story like a colorful bubble, responding to the slightest gust of air. Her gyniconology is informed by the pervasive images of the mindless beauty, or what Barbara Warren calls "the plastic doll."[13]

Galia's most memorable feature is her body: "Her bright hair was streaming like two waves of desire alongside her beautiful, unattainable face. Her white socks gleamed in the dark, moving up and down with the step of her sweet feet, that were treading on my shadow" (A.D., p. 53). These descriptions teach us more about the narrator's passion than about Galia's character. Her "beautiful hair" signifies the narrator's desire, just as her gleaming socks and sweet feet allude metonymically to her tendency to step on him—here on his shadow—throughout the story.

A more explicit link between female beauty and its destructive effects is offered in "The Evening Voyage of Yatir." It would seem that Ziva, the attractive adolescent who causes the derailment of the express train running through the secluded village of Yatir, shares the inhabitants' unrecognized longing to be noticed by the outside world. If it had not been for Ziva's scheme, the routine life of the village would have continued undisturbed. "But she did not think so, not so thought Ziva, she who matured facing the swift train, she who grew beautiful in the

long daily wait for dusk [when the express train traversed the village],
she who collected her schemes in the same sad and tiresome repetition. .
. . whom I secretly loved with all my heart. And because she knows it,
she avoids me and hides away from me" (*A.D.*, p. 12). Like his counterpart in "Galia's Wedding," this protagonist-narrator represses his passion
until he is no longer able to contain it and lets it explode into a destructive action: he joins Ziva in her attempt to convince the village leaders to
bring about an unprecedented "accident" by stopping the express train
in its tracks. Having received the tacit approval of Bardon, the village
secretary, and Mr. Knaot, the supervisor, and unhindered by Arditi, the
old station director (the only one who expresses any resistance to the
plan), the two proceed to execute their plan: "Ziva hurried enthusiastical-
ly towards the red flag . . . quickly untied it and spread it . . . . Ziva put
the red flag in my hand, and I made haste to drop the old green flag, and
with both my hands held the red flag" (p. 26).

Although it would seem that both Ziva and the narrator are responsible for the accident that predictably ensues, it is made clear that the latter is an unwilling accomplice compelled by his passion to act against his
better judgment. Ziva is not only the initiator of the scheme, but is also
visibly more enthusiastic than her besotted follower about the prospect
of bringing about a fatal accident. Despite her enthusiasm, however,
Ziva goes about her plan in a peculiarly absentminded way. Even as she
is unfolding her scheme to the narrator and to the village leaders, she
tends to meander evasively. There is an irreducible vacuity about her
and when the train predictably crashes against the rocks, spilling out its
dead and wounded passengers, Ziva is deeply disturbed and acts like an
innocent outsider: "Pale and trembling she [is] standing, dumbfounded in
front of the actual disaster. I am stretching my arm toward her and
calming her with a light smile: 'Here you are, darling . . . .' But she looks
at me like a stranger. Her lips are moving without words. She is wring-
ing her hands with despair and runs off lightfootedly toward the swarm-
ing wadi" (*A.D.*, p. 27). When he meets her by a dying passenger, the narrator notices that she is sad: Her "sunken eyes were veiled with tears.
With her hand she was caressing lightly the bandaged face of the dying
man" (p. 29). Ziva's absentmindedness characterizes both her attempt to
derail the train and her treatment of the accident casualties. Her description suggests that she is acting out a sort of fantasy rather than participating in a real event. Ziva apparently does not understand the meaning of her schemes and actions. Shortly after the accident takes place,
she is unfolding a new plan to frame Arditi, who objected to her original
desire to derail the train. Like Galia, Ziva appears to be unconscious of
the moral implications of her actions and of the pain she inflicts upon
men.

Several critics have read "The Evening Voyage of Yatir" as an allegory about the State of Israel. Nilli Sadan-Loebenstein suggests that Ziva symbolizes the land.[14] An object of desire whose possession is forever insecure, Ziva, like the land, cannot possibly be aware of the pain she inflicts on those who love her. Much as this interpretation is attractive, it does not and would not explain away the mimetic inadequacies in Yehoshua's gyniconology. Ziva's symbolic aspect would have been just as effective had her mimetic aspect been less stereotypic. The story's symbolic function can neither disguise nor excuse the androcentric premises underlying Ziva's mimetic presentation.

Although Yehoshua's gyniconologies in *Opposite the Forests* (1969) tend to be more plausible, they nevertheless testify to a fundamental inability to understand and depict the inner life of a female character. "Three Days and a Child," which focuses on the character Dov's unrequited and unadmitted love for Haya, the young, gorgeous, and unattainable wife of Ze'ev, may be the best example. While the narrative traces with great sensitivity Dov's jealousy and despair and the way in which all these emotions lead to his perverse subconscious resolution to wreak vengeance on Haya's three-year-old son Yali, it avoids dealing with Haya's motivations.

Like Galia, Haya seems too self-absorbed (or too obtuse?) to realize that Dov is desperately in love with her. Lest we mistake Haya's mute resistance to Dov's amorous attention for an expression of loyalty to Ze'ev, the story makes it clear that Haya had been just as blank long before her marriage. She does not respond to Dov's first timid expressions of love as he cleans the dirt off her feet during vintage session in the kibbutz, "she was silent and continued to be silent. She sat as if [she were] in pain. She did not move from her place, did not draw in her legs. When I got up, desperate, she was still sitting, the pruning-hook dangling from her hand, her eyes wide open." (*A.D.*, p. 214). Haya is just as sluggish and slow to react when, years later, Dov returns to the kibbutz to pay her a visit: "She was reading with her typical dreamy concentration . . . . She noticed me and smiled lightly, as if it were only natural that I should be here in front of her, on a rainy day, two years after I left the kibbutz for good" (*A.D.*, p. 204). Haya's "talent to treat people as if they were inanimate" (p. 204) and "her quietness which might drive others to insanity" (p. 205) remains unchanged when three years later she and Ze'ev put their son Yali in Dov's custody while they are taking entrance examinations at the Hebrew university. Haya remains silent in response to Dov's subtle allusion to his feelings for her: " 'You know, the boy resembles you. All his facial features. In the morning, when I saw him, I got excited...' Her silence" (p. 229). Haya's placidity explains Dov's unconscious decision to avenge himself on her helpless son.

When Yali is delivered into his custody, Dov begins to torture Yali under the guise of a concerned babysitter. Suspecting that the child is feverish, Dov makes things worse by taking Yali to the zoo, the swimming pool, and the playground and by feeding him sweets and icecreams instead of wholesome meals. At one point, the feverish child lies in bed as a poisonous snake—caught by Zvi, an amateur herpetologist and Dov's friend—finds its way out of its box into the child's room.

Dov's sadistic treatment of Haya's son is perverse, yet understandable. Exasperated by his failure to attain his beloved woman, he vents his rage on the child whose features are so reminiscent of hers. It is possible, on the other hand, that Yali signifies for Dov both the product of her intimate contact with another man and a final, unsurpassable obstacle in his quest for her. By destroying Yali, Dov may hope to win her back. Whatever the case, Dov's apparently bizarre conduct is not so bizarre after all. To a large extent, what illuminates it as a deeply human experience are the details we have about Dov's passion for the unavailable Haya. Yet Haya herself remains inscrutable. Her passivity and absentmindedness are presented as obvious givens requiring no further investigation. She remains opaque and mysterious throughout the story, much as she is seen by the protagonist-narrator. Most importantly, Yehoshua's gyniconology deprives Haya of the struggles and conflicts typifying her male counterparts. In this respect, Yehoshua may be reproducing a Western androcentric mythogyny, which Vivian Gornick, for example, describes as follows: "Woman herself is not locked in this profound struggle with the self; she is only the catalyst for man's struggle with himself."[15]

Dov's unrequited love for Haya is paralleled by Zvi's hopeless attachment to Yael, Dov's girlfriend and an indefatigable botanist specializing in thorns. While Haya is largely unaware of Dov's passion, Yael seems aware of Zvi's feelings but is indifferent to them. She lets Zvi follow her around, even when she spends the night with Dov. One may plausibly speculate that Zvi brings a poisonous snake to Dov's apartment in a subconscious attempt to harm his opponent. But like Dov, who ends up hurting himself, Zvi too is finally bitten by his own snake. In both cases, man's love for woman proves to be a self-destructive venture. "Three Days and a Child" may very well be alluding to the animal in woman and man, as is indicated by the names of the main characters (Dov means 'bear'; Haya, 'animal'; Ze'ev, 'wolf'; Zvi, 'deer'; and Yael, 'mountain goat'), but in the encounter between the sexes, the prey tends to be the man. Man is vulnerable because of his susceptibility to intense passion. Woman, on the other hand, is protected simply by her placidity. Thus Dov and Zvi emerge as pathetic and sympathetic victims, while the unscathed, unruffled Haya and Yael are largely uninteresting.

In "Early in the Summer of 1970" (1972), a nameless American daughter-in-law performs the role of the unobtainable object of desire.[16] For the aged and disillusioned Bible teacher, the narrative's nameless protagonist, she is unattainable because she belongs to his son, a historian whom he loves and envies. The foreign daughter-in-law, like the son's research work and style of life, appears both alien and fascinating to the protagonist-narrator, who becomes vaguely aware of her charms as soon as he meets her: "And he [his son] brings forth his wife. [She is] in slacks, a thin girl wrapped with hair, in a worn-out tassled coat. Apparently [she was] one of his students. And she bends over me and smiles with a bright and soft face. [She was] very pretty, at that moment anyway, she seemed so beautiful, touching me with her transparent cool hand."[17]

When the old father receives what will later turn out to be a false notice about his son's death in the war of attrition, he suddenly becomes energized. Despite his ritual mourning for his son's death, the prospect of interpreting or continuing the latter's research and taking over the responsibility for his daughter-in-law and grandson stir him back to life. When it turns out that his son may be alive, the protagonist sets out on a frantic search for his son in the army.

As the focus of the narrative is the age-old struggle between fathers and sons, it is too predictable that the son's wife should be excluded from the heart of the drama. In this modern variation on the *Akedah*, the female character is as dispensable as her counterpart in the biblical version. If it were not for her role as the catalyst of the old man's perverse rejuvenation, I wonder whether Yehoshua would have presented her at all. And since her role as catalyst devolved on her sexual attractiveness, "her completely dishevelled hair," her "bare feet," and her lips "sucking a cigarette" appear to eclipse what we might refer to as her "inner life" (p. 56).

That the daughter-in-law has no understanding of the political or military situation is made slightly more plausible by the fact that she is a foreigner—an American.[18] Largely ignorant of the past which absorbs in different ways both her father-in-law, the Bible teacher, and her husband, the historian, it seems that her perspective—if she has one at all—is hardly worth exploring. These circumstances appear to naturalize the centrality of her body at the expense of her mind, and to validate her presentation as an object of male desire.

Because of its construction, it is probably not surprising that Yehoshua's first novel, *The Lover* (1977), should also include his first partially successful attempt to present the young female object of desire, Dafi, as one capable of feeling and thought. The structure of this multivocal novel, which consists of the apparently unrelated yet complementary monologues of the protagonist Adam, his wife Asya, his daughter Dafi, his Arab worker Naim, Asya's lover Gavriel, and Gavriel's grandmother Vaducha, requires that each of these characters have at least an autonomous point of view. Consequently, the gyniconology of Dafi is richer and more sophisticated than Tamara's in "A Long Summer Day, His Despair, His Wife and His Daughter" (1968), the story which served as the novel's "kernel." For the significance of Dafi does not hinge exclusively on her status as the object of her boyfriend's desperate love or her father's secret passion for her, as is the case with Tamara. Although, like Tamara, Dafi elicits in Adam vague sexual yearnings, and although she too remains mostly beyond the reach of the besotted Naim (except for a short sexual encounter, which signals the end of their relationship), Yehoshua makes an attempt to explain Dafi's motivations independent of her relations with the novel's male characters.

Dafi shares Tamara's tendency to spend most of her day giggling on the phone and gossiping with her girlfriends. Yet Dafi's attachment to Osnat and Tali may be understood as an attempt to gain through them the attention her mother has failed to give her. Like Tamara, Dafi's performance in school leaves much to be desired, but *The Lover* hints that Dafi's academic failure is not merely the result of intellectual limitations, but rather of her realization that Gavriel Arditi serves not only as her mother's research assistant, but also, or rather principally, as her mother's lover. Having returned one day from the beach earlier than usual, Dafi understands for the first time what keeps Gavriel and Asya busy in Asya's locked office. That night she experiences the first in a series of sleepless nights that will further decrease her ability to stay awake in school. "In two days," she reflects, "school begins, and for the first time I don't feel like studying, but I also don't want the [summer] vacation to go on, I don't feel like anything. I return to bed, try to fall asleep, get up again, tension surges in me like electricity in the veins. Nothing like this has ever happened to me."[19]

In view of this attempt to explain Dafi's instability as more than a manifestation of typical female frivolity, it is curious that towards the end of the novel Dafi should emerge once again as the flimsy teenager she first appears to be. In the beginning of the novel, Dafi appears to be little more than a spoiled middle-class Israeli princess concerned exclusively with such weighty matters as her diet, suntan, and highschool gossip. And at the end of the novel, she appears to seduce Naim only to be able to brag to her female friends about her sexual experience: "I said—come be a lover, for I did not want him to hurt [me]. But he already hurt [me]. It was impossible to stop him. Enough, he must stop immediately, [it is] kind of sweet, Mommie. It is impossible to stop him. This is it. I am for sure the first one of all the girls. If Osnat and Tali only knew. That it's good. It's kind of dreamlike, very pleasant inside, this smooth movement" (p. 422).

Dafi's use of the word "lover" suggests that she might be driven by a subliminal wish to imitate [or become] her mother. Since she does not dote on Naim nearly as much as he does on her, it is difficult to explain her decision in romantic terms. Instead, Yehoshua resorts to conventional mythogynies. Dafi wants Naim to "stop immediately," and unaware of the fact that she does nothing to stop him, she appears to be amazed at the fact that Naim does not stop. And like so many women who scream "rape," she forgets that she is willingly cooperating and pretends that "it is impossible to stop him." Though Dafi admits to feelings of pleasure, she is presented as a passive spectator at an act that somebody is doing to her, or in her rather than as a participant. The subjective monologue notwithstanding, the voice emanating from Dafi is that of a man watching or deriving pleasure from a woman's body. A whole range of possible responses is omitted from the scene, from fear to fascination, from guilt to curiosity. Dafi's gyniconology does not permit even in this moment an ability to be emotionally or physically alert.

This fact suggests that Dafi's gyniconology is more indebted to the blank beauty than we first suspected. The absentmindedness of Ziva and Haya reappear in Dafi in the form of acute somnambulism. Similarly, much like her predeccessors, Dafi is unaware of the anguished passion she inspires in her secret lover and is incapable of reciprocating it, even when, like Ziva, she goes through the motions of making love to him. Often driven by unpredictable changes of mood, Dafi differs markedly from Naim in much the same way that her predecessors differed from their male counterpart.

This last point emerges with particular clarity when we consider, for example, the fact that for Naim the sexual encounter with Dafi is not merely a whimsical escapade, but the realization of all his dreams: "This is happiness. This is the outmost end of happiness. There is nothing greater than this, neither is [anything more] necessary" (p. 421). We empathize with Naim's euphoria because we have been privy to his tortured love for Dafi. Because Naim is permitted to have strong feelings and real problems (he is forced by his father to discontinue his education, he must work for a living, he undertakes unpleasant employments for the sake of being close to Dafi, as an Arab Israeli he feels alienated among Israelis and is not quite at home in his Arab village, and he loses his brother, who has undertaken a suicidal anti-Israeli terrorist mission), we cannot dismiss his predicament as easily as we might Dafi's.

The characterization of Dafi does transcend in important ways the restrictive boundaries set by Yehoshua's previous gyniconologies of adolescents. For, unlike her predecessors, Dafi is capable of cognition.

But the role of the female object of desire, with its attendant blankness and passivity, is not altogether missing from the novel. It is immaculately performed by Tali, whose similarity to Dafi suggests that she may be understood as Dafi's double, or foil. Like Dafi, Tali is the product of a shaky marriage, her father having fled from her shrewish mother. The pretty, empty-headed Tali is also a failure at school, and she too shares Dafi's sleepiness, although hers is nowhere explained. It is in fact Tali's tendency to lie down and nap, anywhere, anytime, that attracts Adam to her. One hot day, having entered Dafi's room in search of the morning newspaper, Adam discovers, to his astonishment, Tali asleep in Dafi's bed: "But she does not know that she lay down on the paper, and with a swift movement I lift both her legs, pull the paper which has retained her body's warmth, show it to her with a confused smile. She smiles, closes her eyes and goes back to sleep" (p. 313). While Adam is devoured by "a sense of death mingled with desire" (p. 313). Tali continues to nap, unaware of the commotion she has stirred up. In response to Adam's question, she explains that she is not tired, but says "I always lie down like that." As Adam observes, "she speaks with a strange slowness, as if something is stopped up inside her" (p. 314).

For lack of a better thing to do, Tali begins to follow Adam around, accepting his gifts unquestioningly. When Adam attempts to seduce Tali on the beach, he appears to feel ashamed and confused, at the very least aware of the awkwardness of the situation. Tali, by contrast, remains placid throughout this scene. As Adam, who narrates the scene, puts it: "[She] is inert, like a sort of object. I take off her shirt, smitten by the brightness revealed to me, and underdeveloped girl's chest with its blossoms. I close my eyes and hide them in this childish flesh, moving my lips across her tiny hard breasts, not believing that this is how it is, that it is I who am destroying myself" (p. 322). In this scene, Adam is a man in extremis, devoured by passion and plagued by compunction. His frustrated needs justify his behavior, and his self-consciousness mitigates its objectionability. Even when he takes Tali to Vaducha's hospital (note the thematic link of Eros, sickness, and death) and has intercourse with her, we understand his motives. For, as we shall see, Adam has not been sexually active for a long time; who could blame the poor man who is bored by his wife? Tali, by contrast, is a slow-witted, half-retarded, vacuous object of desire who lacks the elementary capability of feeling, willing, or suffering. Predictably, she falls asleep shortly after her intercourse with Adam. Thus Dafi and Tali respond to their first intercourse with a kind of numbness. There is much in their indifference to their environment which reminds us of their predecessors in Yehoshua's short stories.

Yehoshua's languishing beauties personify the walls against which the male hero beats his head again and again. They may represent the false ideals that his heroes are wrongheadedly pursuing in a vain attempt to find meaning or happiness. The objects of male desire, they lack the ability of their male counterparts to think, to feel, or to act. Their gyniconologies deprive them of the ability to search—even maladroitly or futilely—for their own meaning. Lacking what we might refer to as "consciousness," they also lack the will, the energy, with which to be absurd.

The Inaccessible Wife

If the most exasperating feature of the young beauty is her inability to respond to her lover's desire, the wife's most frustrating aspect is her failure to take care of her husband and children. In both cases, the female in question refuses to perform her expected role: the beauty fails to act in accordance with the hopes her ravishing exterior arouses, while the wife fails to fulfil her duty as a subservient and attentive helpmate or nurturing and supportive mother.[20] While Yehoshua's husbands are caricatured for their failure to lead socially responsible lives, his wives are satirized for shirking their familial duties. The distorting angle underlying Yehoshua's characterization of husbands is based on the premise that man belongs in the world; therefore, his most comic male protagonists are those who are most out of touch with their social and political context.[21] The complementary premise, that woman belongs at home, inspires the comic characterization of his career-oriented wives, who are always too busy to attend to their husbands' needs.

Ruth in "A Long Summer Day, His Despair, His Wife and His Daughter" is a case in point. The busy and absentminded wife of a middle-aged hydrolics engineer, Ruth does not appear to be particularly moved by her husband's return from a nine-month professional trip to Africa on doctor's orders (he is suspected to have cancer). "A quiet Ruth was waiting for him by a fresh glass of tea. There was a deep silence in the universe. Now he wished to begin to tell [her] about the hospital, but she stopped him immediately. Not now. Tomorrow. If he insists on speaking, let him talk about something else, perhaps about the dam."[22] Ruth avoids discussing her husband's physical condition or state of mind. Although she demonstrates technical dexterity with the necessary procedures for checking him into the hospital and out of it, when his growth proves to be nonmalignant she remains emotionally detached: "Ruth arrived in the afternoon, ran about for several hours from one office to the next, collected a huge bundle of documents, the results of medical examinations, him and his suitcase. She was in a great hurry" (p. 164). the absence of any distinction between the husband and the other items Ruth is busily collecting from the hospital, the reference to the husband as one of the last items on her list, and her apparent indifference to her husband's release from the hospital indicate the businesslike distance she keeps from her husband.

Not only is Ruth unresponsive to her husband's emotional needs, but she also rejects his sexual advances. Her gentle but firm rejection of his attempt to make love to her on the evening of his arrival home foreshadows her behavior throughout the narrative: "He embraced her; despite his overwhelming exhaustion, he wanted to be with her, throw her on the bed, and sleep with her, if only to prove that he is still alive. But she pushed him away lightly, kissed him on the head, took off her clothes, put on her nightgown and went to bed" (p. 163). When pressed by her husband, she makes a lame excuse, referring to her exhaustion and preoccupation with her courses. Yehoshua's ironic use of the narrated monologue emphasizes the spuriousness of Ruth's arguments: "But he sees himself, she is dying of exhaustion, and a pitiless week is awaiting her. Yes [this is] a crazy period. She will finish her studies and examinations, and then . . ." (p. 170). It is not quite clear whether Ruth uses her activities as excuses, or whether they indeed deplete her of the emotional and sexual energy she is expected to invest in her husband. What is clear is that Ruth's professional aspirations are inimical to her uxorial and maternal duties.

Ruth's somnambulant response to her husband's needs on the night of his arrival is an eloquent metaphor for her general attitude toward him. Failing to realize that it is her own placidity that is the source of her husband's insomnia, Ruth resorts to a rather superficial solution: "She was quiet. Suddenly she got up, with closed eyes she searched for her slippers, went like a somnambulist to the bathroom, [and] returned with a glass of water and sleeping pills in her hand" (p. 163). This scene foreshadows the way in which Ruth treats her husband throughout the narrative. For it is indeed with "closed eyes" that she responds to his needs, dragging her heels sleepily, remaining utterly inaccessible to his silent and explicit pleas. She offers her husband soporifics rather than curative medicine, much as she employs evasive strategies and stopgap measures in dealing with his demands. "Like a somnambulist" —mechanically and absentmindedly—she performs her role as wife.

While we do not know what is behind Ruth's flight from reality, we are made aware of the extent to which "His Wife" is the cause of "His

Despair." For it is clearly Ruth's inattentiveness to his problems, and excessive absence from home, that ultimately drives the jobless, disoriented protagonist to destroy the budding relationship between his adolescent daughter Tamara and her boyfriend Gadi. The wife's inaccessibility functions as an important factor in the motivation of the protagonist. But what may explain Ruth's obtuseness?

The wife's apathy assumes lurid national and political implications when contextualized in a narrative like "Missile Base 612" (1975). Here the indifference of the sleepy wife toward her husband connotes an indifference toward the nation state. The nameless male protagonist is fulfilling his national military duty as he plods through Missile Base 612, while his wife remains detached from whatever represents the public sphere. This is not to say that the husband embodies a model Israeli citizen. He is neither enthusiastic about the prospect of performing his military duty, nor is he genuinely interested in the topics he is planning to discuss as part of his duty. But while his stagnant relationship with his wife is presented as the single most important cause of his despondency, we are not given any clues as to her somnambulism. All we know is that the wife has given up her sexual interest in her husband ("this masturbation alone at night" *A.D.* p. 275), her maternal duty ("the child is also growing lonely"), and her obligations as a homemaker ("he is warming the food he prepared for himself in the beginning of the week," *A.D.* p. 258)—all of which are considerable irritants to her husband.

The inaccessible wife continues to sleep even when her husband is preparing to go off to the army: "He enters the bedroom to take his reservist uniform and is astonished to see her still asleep in the dark, in the same diagonal, nocturnal position, her face calm as if time has come to a stop" (*A.D.*, p. 258). And indeed, time for this female character has come to a stop. No matter how inadequate her husband's participation in the sociopolitical scene, he is at least presented as experiencing time, Israeli time. Yehoshua's gyniconology, however, deprives the protagonist's wife of this privilege. In this respect, Yehoshua does not differ from many of his Western counterparts' creations who, as Martha and Charles Masinton put it, "are exempt from the burden of contemporaneity and allowed refuge either in myth or in stereotypical female roles."[23]

The protagonist's awkward relationship with his wife explains his confusion and his despair. His anxiety over his neglected son explains his inability to perform his national duty properly. We understand that there is a direct correlation between his sexual frustration and the advances he makes at his chauffeur, a giant of a soldier girl who appalls and disgusts him. The protagonist's domestic problems also illuminate his erotic attraction to the missiles:

> From time to time he stops to observe the missile pits, examines them.
> This insipidity, the futility, the boredom, the imminent divorce, this
> masturbation alone at night, the child who is corroded between the two
> of them. And suddenly, with an unexpected decision he looks about to
> make sure no one is in sight, he alights into the bottom of one of the pits
> determined to feel the missiles with his own hands. And here they are
> in front of him, directed toward the bright skyline, dim, pinkish. He
> touches them cautiously, astonished to find them a bit smooth, wet, as if
> covered with a light oil, or a whitish dew (A.D. p. 275).

The protagonist's perverse attraction to the penis-shaped, "dim, pinkish,"
"smooth, wet" missiles is presented as a questionable substitute for a
heterosexual relationship with his wife. The tension between the protagonist and his wife may explain this perverse substitution. The inaccessible wife drives her sexually frustrated husband to a grotesque affair
with military weapons. Is not the wife, then, the ultimate cause of the
male fascination with weapons and wars?

Just as the military base is suffused with erotic undertones, the
strained marital relationship is described in military terms: "For several
months now he has not exchanged a word with his wife. The first shots
were fired a long time ago. The causes are unclear now; at present they
are in an open state of war" (A.D., p. 254). "He will return home ready
for battle" (A.D. p. 285). The reversal works both ways: marriage has
turned into a war of attrition, just as the battlefield has been trans-
formed into an erotic playground.

Though he may not be aware of it, the protagonist partially embodies the title of one of the lectures he routinely gives as part of his
reserve duty: "Israeli Society in an Ongoing Struggle." His neurotic
behavior is the result of his ongoing struggle with his wife. That
Yehoshua is interested in the relationship between the individual's conduct and national warfare is made clear by his essay, "The Individual and
Society in an Ongoing Struggle."[24] Within this context, what is the function of the sleepy wife? What may she represent? I would like to suggest
that the sleepy wife embodies the obstacle of the male individual and
society, that which deprives both of peace and happiness. The
wife's significance is restricted to her destructive impact on her husband. This fact may explain why her gyniconology does not give us any
details about her Self. Since her most important role is to represent the
real enemy of the male individual and of society, there is no need for any
details about her own motivations.

The insipid relationship of Adam and Asya in The Lover is also
presented against the background of a military conflict, here the Yom
Kippur War of 1973. The couple's marital conflict seems to eclipse the

impact of the military conflict, although this reversal of priorities serves, among other things, to undermine the validity of their set of values. If Gavriel had not disappeared shortly after his induction to the army, Asya and Adam may hardly have noticed that a devastating war had broken out. If Gavriel had not disappeared from the army, Asya would have continued with her teaching and her extramarital affair with Gavriel, and Adam would have continued expanding his garage. That the couple perceives the war as a trivial detail largely ancillary to their "real" interests may be closely related to their inability to relate to each other. The thematic link between warfare and the couple's silent antagonism alludes to a possible causal relationship between the couple's arid marriage and their indifference to the national predicament.

But even though both Adam and Asya are afflicted with a kind of emotional numbness, Asya's numbness seems more severe. Asya is incapable of asking the hard questions Dafi and Adam occasionally ask about the Arab-Israeli conflict and the meaning of Zionism. Watching some of his Arab employees, Adam wonders about the inevitable conflict experienced by Arab Israelis: "to live in this reality and to live also its opposite" (p. 189). Asya, by contrast, is oblivious to these problems, although one would expect that her training as a history highschool teacher should deepen her interest in them. She does not deal with Dafi's confused question about Zionist history during one of the guest lectures she gives in Dafi's class. We also do not know whether she has thought about the problem of suicidal terrorism which crops up during one of her peers' soirees.

Asya's unawareness of the deteriorating political situation complements and parallels her blindness to the growing degeneration of her marital life. She seems to be too busy with her professional obligations to notice the change in Adam, whereas he is forebodingly aware of the growing chasm between them. While she never bothers to think of her husband or his needs, he continuously attempts to understand what went wrong in their relationship: "But how should I describe her? Where should I begin?" (p. 68). "I am constantly observing my wife, examining her from a side, with a stranger's eye . . . Is it still possible to fall in love with her?" (p. 91). Unlike the protagonist-narrator of "A Long Summer Day," Adam is no longer interested in his aging wife, "a gray woman, white in her hair, in an old gown, in flat slippers" (p. 26).

Asya, like Ruth, is unaware of her husband's frustration, although she appears to sense his sexual disinterest. When Adam provides her with Gavriel, she accepts it gratefully. She does not appear to be disturbed by her husband's tacit encouragement of her affair. Neither does she seem to mind the impact her affair with Gavriel might have on Dafi.

Unlike Adam, she rarely questions the meaning of her life or her relationship with her family and friends. When Gavriel disappears, she lets
Adam do the searching, only half aware that Dafi and Naim also participate in the nocturnal searches for her lover. Like Ruth in "A Long
Summer Day," and the sleepy wife in "Missile Base 612," Asya is deeply
asleep while her husband spends restless nights in pursuit of false solutions to his deadlocked marriage. As with other wives, this somnolence
seems to be chronic. Adam notes: "Asya is asleep. It is impossible to have
a rational contact with her. When I wake her up, she does respond, she
talks, but she does not get up, and just as I turn my head, she falls asleep
again" (p. 274). Asya's somnolent response to her husband emblematizes
her general inaccessibility.

Asya's indifference exasperates Dafi as well: "For my mother is absent. I grasped it last year; my mother is absent even when she is at
home, and if one really wants to have a quiet, heart to heart talk with
her, one must ask for [an appointment] a week in advance" (p. 43). But
Dafi never succeeds in having the desirable "quiet, heart to heart" talk
with her busy and absentminded mother. In a subconscious retaliation
against her mother's indifference, Dafi begins to neglect her studies. Her
awareness of her mother's affair with Gavriel robs her of her ability to
sleep. But Asya, who teaches in Dafi's highschool, is not even aware of
her daughter's imminent expulsion, and when she learns about it, she
reacts rather placidly. Ironically, it is Adam and not Asya, who tries in
vain—by offering to service the principal's wrecked car—to prevent
Dafi's expulsion from school.[25]

The only talk Dafi has with Asya occurs shortly after Asya is
awakened from a nightmarish dream about Dafi. This rare conversation
ends with Asya's slapping Dafi across the face: "She hit me. Perhaps for
seven years she did not touch me, and [now] I am beginning to calm
down, I am relieved. My cheek is burning, tears are bursting into my
eyes, but something has opened up in me from this slap, an exhaustion,
something in me is thawing away" (p. 343). Dafi prefers her mother's
violent gesture and the physical pain it causes to the cold detachment
she has experienced throughout the years. For shortly after this rare encounter between mother and daughter, Dafi falls asleep. To the extent
that Asya's slap is expressive of maternal concern, its overwhelming effectiveness makes psychological sense, in addition to being comic. If
"perhaps for seven years" Dafi was not touched by her mother, it is not
difficult to guess why this rare physical contact should be able to cure
her of her insomnia.

What is less clear is what prevents Asya from experiencing and expressing anything like love or concern for Dafi and Adam. Why is Asya,

who is otherwise intelligent, so insensitive to her family's needs? Why is this highschool teacher barely capable of rational thinking or intellectual speculation? If consciousness may be imagined as a receptacle of feelings and thoughts, why does Asya's appear to be so hopelessly empty of both? Since the multivocal framework of *The Lover* eliminates the structural co-optation by a male protagonist narrator of the female point of view, we should expect to have greater access to the hitherto unknown inner world of Yehoshua's female characters. Since all the novel's characters are introduced to us through long internal monologues, we should expect to know as much about Asya as we know about Adam. But we do not. For while Adam's internal monologues describe intentions, actions, calculated plans, and seething emotions—a wide array of rational and ir-rational activities, both speculative and actual—Asya's monologues describe almost exclusively her dreams. We are expected to reconstruct Asya's oneiric images and narratives in such a way as to make them at least partially intelligible mediators of her otherwise suppressed thoughts and feelings.

Asya's dreamworld reveals that the sleepy wife is more than a two-dimensional automaton, that she does have fears and desires of her own. Asya's nightmares about Dafi, for example, indicate that she does care for and worry about her daughter. Her dream about Dafi's near rape by a strange murderer (pp. 40–42), and about Dafi's grotesque impregnation by wheat seeds (pp. 329–330) allude to Asya's anxiety about Dafi's sexual vulnerability. Her dream about her dead firstborn son Yigal (pp. 225–226) reveals that, contrary to what her apparently quick recovery may have indicated, his death continues to bother her. These dreams also reveal a measure of suppressed hostility against Adam, who seems peculiarly helpless and placid in these oneiric contexts. One may say that, in her dreams, Asya reverses roles with Adam, allotting to him the role of the negligent parent she performs in real life. Asya's dream about defec-tive pregnancies and babies (pp. 58–59, 329–330) may, on the other hand, also be interpreted as a reflection of her deep-seated resistance to reproduction and maternity.

And then there are, of course, Asya's erotic dreams about real and imaginary men. She dreams about a boy with a striking resemblance to Yitzhak (the immigrant boy who was in love with her in highschool) tak-ing off his clothes in her classroom (pp. 106–107). She dreams about Gavriel as a medical assistant, forcing open her mouth and exploring it with "a thin ruler," causing her to feel "inundated with pleasure" (p. 139). She dreams about an all-too-short encounter with an aggressive, masculine Gavriel while cooking a "huge, wild fish" (a symbol of fertility?) In this dream, she is "trembling with hope that he touch her" and thinks, "perhaps I could embrace him" (p. 289). She dreams about "an enormous, very elegant black man" showing her through a gallery of live pictures of "a fertile and rich landscape" (pp. 276–277).

The least Asya's dreams reveals is that beneath her stolid posture hides a seething sea of fears and desires. The prim and proper highschool teacher is not as boring and gray as her clothes and hair may lead us to believe. A possible answer to our query about Asya's inaccessibility and apparent insipidity is that she suppresses her feelings and thoughts. Her monologues do not address those feelings because she is not (or refuses to be) conscious of them. But to say that Asya dreams so much because she does not wish to confront her fears and desires is begging the question. For the real queston is why the author preferred to present the wife through highly suggestive, elusive dreams. Why did he deprive Asya of a conscious and self-conscious mind?

Considered connotationally, Asya's dreamworld validates the idea that woman's central preoccupations are sex and procreation. Asya's subconscious life suggests that a woman's professional pursuits are ancillary to her sexual needs. Thus her gyniconology seems to be inspired by the misogynist prejudice about woman's inherent limitations. As Otto Weininger put it: "The condition of sexual excitement is the supreme moment of a woman's life. The woman is devoted wholly to sexual matters, that is to say, to the spheres of begetting and reproduction. Her relations to her husband and children complete her life, whereas the male is something more than sexual.[26]

It may be that by opting for the murky, ambiguous world of dreams as the major expressive mode of Asya's inner life, Yehoshua has opted for a facile mythogynous strategy. From an artistic point of view, it is surely less problematic to let "your heroine float out there, just like that, unclear, unresolved, as the fictional critic Saul Levin says to Dina, another one of Yehoshua's inaccessible wives who appear in *Late Divorce*.[27]

But Yehoshua's gyniconological focus on the oneiric image in *The Lover* may represent more than just a facile artistic strategy. It may also be read as an implicit endorsement of the idea that woman is more susceptible than man to murky, incoherent thinking. In Otto Weininger's words: "With the woman, thinking and feeling are identical . . . Woman is sentimental, and knows emotion but not mental excitement."[28] Yael in *Late Divorce* is another wife incapable of cogitation. Asi, her brother, wonders: "Does she ever think? Yael, think! We used to beg her when she suddenly got stuck" (p. 134). Her own monologue reflects her effort to reconstruct the events of a forgotten day, which she is apparently incapable of analyzing, ("I am with you, I am with everybody") or of judging ("I will remember. You will do the thinking for me") (p. 231).[29]

To return to *The Lover*, the gyniconology of Vaducha, Gavriel's old grandmother, is also suggestive of the alleged inseparability of woman's thinking and feeling. Throughout most of the novel, Vaducha is comatose. Her state of mind is introduced to the reader through a series of metonymic images. Thus, her first internal monologue, describing a stone, signals the beginning of Vaducha's emergence from her prolonged coma: "A stone rests on a white sheet. A large stone. One turns a stone over, washes a stone, feeds a stone and the stone urinates slowly" (p. 24). The second monologue, describing the development of a plant into an animal (p. 99), and the third, describing a patient's escape from a hospital to a field (or an orchard) (p. 150), metonymically depict Vaducha's gradual transformation from an unconscious, inanimate object into a cognating person. She regains consciousness and returns to her home, only to relapse shortly afterwards into sickness and to expire towards the end of the novel.

Except for a few delightfully comic interchanges between Vaducha and Naim, who is hired by Adam as her babysitter, Vaducha's characterization lacks specificity to such an extent that one is compelled to justify her existence in the novel on the basis of her possible symbolic function.[30] And, indeed, several "facts" about Vaducha's life do lend themselves to symbolic interpretation. For we are told that she was born in 1882, the historic date which witnessed the establishment of the Zionist movement, and that she survived a severe illness in 1948, when Israel won its war of independence against the Arabs. Vaducha finally dies toward the end of the Yom Kippur War of 1973. As other critics have noticed, there is too much correlation between Vaducha's biography and that of the socialist Zionist movement or, in more general terms, the land of Israel. Deserted by her grandson Gavriel (as the country is by Israeli expatriates), and kept alive by Naim (an allusion to the importance of Arab labor for the upkeep of the country?), Vaducha serves as an effective tool in the novel's critique of Israel's loss of its commitment to the original socialist Zionist vision.[31]

But the effectiveness of Vaducha's symbolic aspect cannot answer for the problem of her mimetic presentation. Vaducha remains an unresolved half-symbol, much like the middle-aged schizophrenic Naomi in *Late Divorce*. The "wild" and "primitive" image Naomi sees hovering in the air (pp. 264, 273, 275, 279) may perhaps signify, as some critics have suggested, the uncultivated land of Israel to whom the Jewish pioneers (symbolized by Naomi's husband Yehuda) swore allegiance. But, like Vaducha, Naomi fails in a mimetic sense. Her insanity seems inherent and remains a mystery, whereas the neurosis of Yehuda is more convincing and therefore more moving. While Yehuda, out of the enormous pressure of his guilt and anxiety over Naomi, goes momentarily insane, Naomi, we are told, is constitutionally mad. As Yosef Oren puts it, "There is no explanation for Naomi's schizophrenic state in the novel other than the political historical one."[32]

It may be that in opting for obtuseness, sleepiness, dreaminess, anility, or madness, Yehoshua, like other male Israeli authors, avoids a more serious examination of his gyniconologies. In this case, he may not differ much from Dina in *Late Divorce*, who decides, in response to Mr. Levin's critique to "make her heroine a bit primitive, perhaps half crazy, so it will be easier to motivate her" (p. 102). On the other hand, one may speculate that the frequent presentation of female consciousness as primitive or defective draws on the idea that women are cognitively inferior to men. The omission in Yehoshua's fiction of plausible gyniconologies suggests an implicit appeal to traditional androcentric perceptions of women as intellectually or cognitively inferior to men. Though Yehoshua himself may not be faulted with a conscious endorsement of the idea that "the female is soulless and possesses neither ego nor individuality, personality nor freedom, character nor will," his mythogynies do not appear to challenge it in any way.[33]

Summary

The trajectory of Yehoshua's female character from youth to old age seems to affirm Ellen Morgan's observation about women in traditional novels: "Women matured physically, at which point they were ripe for being loved. Then they deteriorated physically, at which point they either disappeared from sight in the novel or became stereotypes. Once physically mature, they were thought to have reached the peaks of their potential and development, which were defined in physical rather than spiritual, intellectual or emotional terms."[34] While Yehoshua's young women are unattainable beauties, his mature women are either frigid or undesirable. In either case, the female character is defined in terms of her physical attractiveness to her male counterpart(s).

Anchored in her inescapable "female nature," Yehoshua's fictional woman has no access to, or understanding of, the more significant struggles carried on by men. Not that the men are heroic role models. But no matter how awkward their ventures, they nevertheless interact with their society, and most importantly, they are *conscious* (though often inadequately) of the unresolvable dilemma or obsession which haunts them. Because of their defective cognitive capabilities, Yehoshua's female characters are debarred from struggles of larger existential or national meaning. At best, they serve as symbolic representations of a beloved but treacherous country, a land resistant to the desperate wooing of her sons and lovers.

In *The Lover*, as well as in *Late Divorce*, Yehoshua does go beyond the stereotypic confines of the *belle dame sans merci* and the inaccessible wife. The least we can say is that in his later works he wrests his female characters from their previous marginality. Nevertheless, by focusing on the absentmindedness of the young beauty, the somnambulism of the middle-aged wife, and the anility of the old woman, Yehoshua does not go too far beyond the restrictive gyniconologies of the major Palmah authors. Furthermore, by opting for oneiric images and comatose states as his most frequent means of female characterization, Yehoshua implicitly validates the traditional androcentric visions of femininity as Otherness.

CHAPTER 4

Amos Oz:
The Lack of Conscience

In her monograph on Amos Oz, Nurith Gertz points out correctly that, despite its various permutations, the author's fiction revolves around a perennial conflict between "the realm of goodness, the civilized, the unsatisfactory, and the realm of evil, the wild, the destructive, the seductive."[1] In this context, the kibbutz, which often serves as a metaphoric microcosm of the state of Israel, corresponds to the regulated, routinized, and pedestrian realm of civilization, whereas the surrounding Arab territories, the dark, uncultivated expanses dominated by predatory animals (in *Where the Jackals Howl*), by Germany (in *Elsewhere Perhaps*), or by other European countries (in *The Hill of Evil Counsel*) often correspond to the luring yet sinister world of desire and death. It is not merely that an enchanting "dark and irrational world surrounds the person all around," as Gershon Shaked says.[2] The would-be civilized island is itself teeming with irrational desires. The conflict between culture and nature, reason and passion rages inside the civilized island (and the civilized mind) as it does on the border separating it from the outside.

What has not been noticed yet, however, is that the primary representatives of the internal forces threatening to break up the civilized social unit or civilized mind are women. While male characters are often torn asunder by opposite attractions to nature and culture, female characters are the exclusive vehicles of nature. Chaos and nature often beckon to male characters in the guise of seductive women. Incapable of appreciating the value of civilized life and unhindered by any moral principles, responsibility, or commitment to ideals or people, Oz's female characters experience civilized life as an oppressive routine from which they often successfully attempt to escape. The "hero" who "tries to break out of a desolate reality through violent action," as Gertz puts it, is more often than not a heroine.[3]

If Gertz is right in positing that Oz's hero personified Israel's desperate attempt to make contact with the outside world through war, the gynomorphic representation of violence becomes doubly significant. As the direct or indirect cause of malaise in the civilized context, the female character parallels and complements the attempt of the external forces to intrude into the society and destroy it. Her desire to break out of civilized society and to unite with the seductive and destructive outsiders reveals her as an Other who has more in common with external Others than with her own society. While Oz's heroines are frustrated romantics yearning to break out of the national boundaries, most of their male counterparts tend to represent rather balanced, often "square," individuals who learn to accept reality rather than repudiate it. His few mad heroes suffer from too strong an attachment to the national Self. The nameless hero of "Mending the World" (1964) and Shraga Unger of *Late Love* (1970) are paranoid nationalistic ideologues motivated by an excessive concern for Israel's safety and integrity. Idealism rather than biology dictates their conduct. Eccentric loners, they lack the heroines' capacity to harm anyone but themselves.

This is not to say that Oz's authorial irony spares his male fanatics. Neither does it spare the tolerant and optimistic male counterparts of his destructive heroines (such as Reuven Harish in *Elsewhere Perhaps*, Michael Gonen in *My Michael*, and Hans Kipnis in "The Hill of Evil Counsel"). Yet, as we shall see, the selfish and destructive heroines who refuse to renounce their vainglorious delusions are the most frequent victims of Oz's most scathing irony. This should come as no surprise to the readers of Oz's political essays, which often satirize expressions of extremism and high expectations of any kind.[4] To the extent that Oz's heroines may be seen as semiotic representations of a nation gone awry (the national Self turned Other), their romantic dreams may allude to the different messianic expectations of extremist Zionist visionaries who demand "that we be 'the most'—[perfect of all], and if not, let us all go to hell. [We must be] 'the most' pure, or socialist, or devout, or sophisticated, or strong, or smart, or 'creative'—each [ideological] trend and its burning demand."[5] As one of the foremost authors of what Amos Elon calls "the Generation of the Sons," Oz gives expression to the discomfort of native Israelis with the messianic expectations of the "Founding Fathers" of modern Israel.[6]

Though it is true that Oz's handling of point of view is more complex than that of his predecessors, I think it is wrong to conclude that with the omniscient point of view of the Palmah authors disappeared also "the assumption that it is possible to say objectively anything truthful about reality" or that Oz's complex and shifting techniques of focalization imply "that it is impossible to have absolute knowledge and it is impossible to judge unilaterally."[7] This conclusion identifies structural complexity with ideological agnosticism. Furthermore, it identifies the ideological disorientation of the characters and unreliable narrators with the implied author's perspective. Yet it is precisely through a posture of false neutrality that the described events and characters are satirized. Though the authorial judgment in Oz in particular, and in the New Wave fiction in general, is less accessible or explicit, it is not completely absent. It cannot be absent in a blatantly sensationalistic text dwelling on familial and social scandals whose moral and national objectionability—especially where female characters are involved—is unambiguous. The unacceptability of Geula's attempt to falsely accuse an innocent Bedouin of rape, Eva Harish's escape from a kibbutz to post–World War II Germany, or Hana Gonen's subversive phantasies about the destruction of Jerusalem with the help of Palestinian terrorists are by no means borderline manifestations of human weakness. The fact is, as we shall see, that the narratives describing the heroines' antisocial behavior present that behavior not only as unforgivable, but as deeply dangerous and essentially inhuman. The muddled point of view of the unreliable narrator or heroine does elicit irony and creates distance.

Oz's unreliable narrators should not be interpreted exclusively as symptomatic of a general breakdown of the fundamental axiologies of the Palmah Generation. What they and the disoriented protagonists often demonstrate is the laughability, the insipidity, of a value-free or uncommitted perspective. Oz's tendency to parody the poetic norms of the Palmah Generation does not imply a rejection of socialist Zionist values. By presenting the actions of a deluded heroine through her own or a would-be objective narrator's point of view, the author dramatizes the tortuous process of self-delusion and the mechanisms of a false consciousness.

My reference to the heroine as the primary perpetrator of morally questionable actions stem from the perennial inability of Oz's female characters to distinguish right from wrong. Male characters may err, but, as we shall see, they often question the moral validity of their actions and motivations, they regret, they retract their steps, and they often change and develop. The female characters, who seem to lack the conscience and the value system necessary for this self-examination, also lack the capacity to experience conflict or to develop in a meaningful or positive way.

Where the Jackals Howl: Woman as Sex

Amos Oz's first collection of stories, *Where the Jackals Howl* (1965), appears to be interested in the behavior of people in extremis. Yet, it is not quite precise to explain the often bewildering lack of believability in his characterization as exclusively the result of archetypalism, as Gershon Shaked suggests.[8] Although I agree with Shaked that it would be wrongheaded to adopt an *exclusively* mimetic approach to Oz's characters, my understanding is that it would be remiss to exclude a mimetic approach from a critical examination of his characterization. The fact is that the 1975 edition of *Where the Jackals Howl* reflects Oz's own attempt to add realistic detail to his plots and develop his characters more plausibly.

A careful consideration of the book's first edition reveals that Oz's gyniconologies emphasize sex. To be sure, the sexual drive does play a role in his characterization of men, but it is usually accompanied by a variety of other psychological drives. Female characters like the adolescent beauty Galila, in the title story, the old widow Batya Pinsky in "A Hollow Stone," the ugly "old maid" Geula in "Nomads and Viper," the middle-aged divorcee, Lily Danenberg in "Strange Fire," the soldier girl Bruria in "The Trappist Monastery" and Tova, the sick poet in "All the Rivers,"—all seem obsessed with their sexual needs, whether they express or suppress them. There is no female counterpart to Gideon Shenhav, the victimized son in "The Way of the Wind"; to Dov Sirkin, the guilt-ridden father in "Before His Time"; or to the frustrated old idealist in "Mending the World." It is not that the male characters are indifferent to sex, it is rather that they are never as completely controlled, consumed, defined by it, as their female counterparts. Oz's gyniconologies use sex as an organizing principle.

Gideon Shenhav, the hero of "The Way of the Wind," is a young kibbutz member, not much younger than Geula of "Nomads and Viper." Both die an untimely death on the premises of their native kibbutz. But whereas Gideon's death—and life, for that matter—is only marginally related to his sexual identity, Geula's life *and* death are strictly determined by hers.

Gideon Shenhav is electrocuted when, during a parachuting parade, his parachute is caught in the electric wires of his kibbutz. The story implies that, in addition to fear and panic, what causes Gideon to jump unto the electric wire, instead of cutting off his parachute straps may have been his refusal to be saved by the fearless Zaki, his teenage brother: "With wide-open eyes, Gideon stared at the vulpine teeth protruding from Zaki's mouth. Terror seized him, as if he was looking into a distorted mirror and saw his own image being effaced."[9] On a deeper level, Gideon may be terrified of what he recognizes to be the "vulpine" image of virility which his father, Shimshon Sheinbaum, has tried all his life to hoist on him. His rejection of Zaki's help entails a rejection of his father's attempt to groom him as a model soldier, fearless and self-reliant. Suspended above his native kibbutz, Gideon vaguely realizes the more significant distance which separates him from his own community as he takes in the distorted faces and jeering remarks of the onlookers and the patronizing instructions and angry shame of his father. The inadequate and insensitive response of the kibbutz community to Gideon's predicament justifies the latter's semiconscious desire to separate himself from them forever.[10] In addition to parodying the heroic protagonist of the Palmah Generation, the description of Gideon's death questions the validity of the image of the kibbutz as a model community. By presenting his death as the direct outcome of a military parade, the narrative points up the vapid showiness, futility, and even danger of such events, thereby critiquing the militaristic ethos in Israel in general.

Geula's death is also a wasteful one, but in very different ways and with largely different implications. The pimply "old maid" dies of a viper's bite as she lies among the shrubs convulsed with frustrated lust.[11] The description of the homely heroine implies that she is sexually frustrated because no one will come near her: "Geula, a thin and short girl, is twenty-nine years old. Even though she hasn't found a husband yet, one cannot deny her commendable attributes, such as her dedication to social and cultural affairs. Her face is thin and pale. No one among our girls can rival her [ability to] brew coffee, real coffee. Two bitter lines run down both corners of her mouth . . . On the hot and humid days, sweat ravages her face and brings out the pimples strewn all over it" (1965, p. 31).

The references to Geula's unattractive physique which interrupt the flow of the narrator's praise, in addition to the evasive generalization concerning her "dedication to social and cultural affairs" and the trivial nature of her "commendable attributes" (brewing coffee), betray the ironic distance of the participant narrator. This ironic distance is maintained throughout the narrative and reaches a certain climax in the description of Geula's encounter with a Bedouin pilferer in the kibbutz orchard. The description gives away Geula's sexual excitement and her barely suppressed hope that the Bedouin will approach her sexually. But the Bedouin's gestures betray no sexual interest. Much like S. Yizhar's disarmingly innocent Arab shepherd in "The Prisoner," he is mostly interested in his sheep and goats. Like the former, he smokes a cigarette with his interlocutor, perhaps in an attempt to appease her, to forestall a vindictive plan, or to gain time. Aware of the tense relations between the kibbutz and the Bedouin pilferers, it is possible that our anonymous shepherd is trying through friendly conversation to dissuade Geula from informing the kibbutz leadership of his illegal poaching on the orchard. By saying that he is too young to be married (although he is clearly an adult man), he may also be hinting that he is sexually unavailable. Geula's semiconscious attempt to seduce the exotic descendant of Adam in this modern version of the Garden of Eden fails miserably. It is not clear whether, stung by her failure, she decides to avenge herself on the Bedouin, or whether she actually deludes herself into believing that the Bedouin tried to rape her. What is clear is that, as she returns to her room to prepare herself for her usual task—serving coffee to the executive committee—she is planning to accuse the pilferer of rape.

What intercepts Geula's plan is her sudden impulse to rest up by some rose bushes. As she lies down, convulsed with sexual lust and frustration, she is bitten by a viper: "A shiver of pleasure runs through her skin. Now she is listening to the sweet wave which penetrates her body and intoxicates her blood. With complete abandonment Geula responds to the sweet wave . . . The pleasure inundates the girl and imbues her with soothing coolness. She is still caressing with her fingers a dry twig. Her fingers are very soft, soft and full of pleasure" (1965, pp. 40–41). Even as death conquers it, the female body is still susceptible, it would seem, to sexual sensations. Geula experiences the circulation of the lethal poison in her veins as a kind of orgasmic ecstasy. Death is her final release from the fetters of sexual desire and her worthless life. Ironically, she achieves through death what she could not achieve by remaining alive.

With Geula dies her plot to incite the kibbutz against the Bedouin poachers.[12] There is thus something redeeming after all in Geula's death. The archetypal thematic cluster of woman, garden and snake implies that this time this Eve—overcome by the poison of her own lust—fails in undermining the human race. Redemption—which is the meaning of Geula's name—was brought to the kibbutz despite, not because of, Geula. As noted earlier, Geula may be driven by self-delusion, or a subliminal attempt to prove her desirability, rather than by malice. But this motivation does not mitigate the fact that it is the female Other who threatens the tenuous relationship between the nation—embodied by the kibbutz—and the national Others. Because of her attraction to those Others, the female Other desires to break out of her community or to undermine its moral integrity.

While Gideon is sacrificed by the kibbutz to the questionable idol of military prowess, Geula is prepared to sacrifice the interests of the kibbutz, to instigate war, to placate her raging sexuality, or soothe her offended pride. Gideon's death serves as a powerful critique of the national Self; Geula's death dramatizes the self-destruction of the national Self. Gideon is an innocent and pathetic victim of a misguided ethos; Geula is a symbol of libidinal and destructive powers, the object rather than the means of Oz's critique of the kibbutz. Her culpability deprives her of Gideon's tragic stature; her stereotypy denies her the empathy elicited by Gideon's characterization.

A quick comparison of Gideon Shenhav, the soft-hearted paratrooper, with Bruria, the ineffective soldier girl in "The Trappist Monastery," also highlights the sexual emphasis in Oz's gyniconologies. Although she is presented as a soldier girl, Bruria's military responsibilities are eclipsed by her sexual exploits. When her boyfriend Itche sets out with his batallion on a reprisal mission against a terrorist base, Bruria finds time to have intercourse with Nahum, the orderly, and later, when Itche returns from the mission, she has intercourse with Rosenthal, the officer. While the original narrative does not explore Bruria's motives, the revised version, by stressing Itche's coarseness, alludes to the possibility that Bruria's "adulterousness" is fueled by vindictiveness and not only by sexual appetite. But, as Nurith Gertz points out, the most significant revisions in the new edition concern the relationship between the male characters Itche and Nahum.[13] Thus even in the revised version, Bruria emerges as essentially a sexual being, her role as a soldier remaining completely incidental to her "true" female nature.[14]

The association of female sexuality, the lack of conscience, and national Otherness emerges most clearly in the characterization of the German immigrant and depraved divorcee Lily Danenberg, the protagonist of "Strange Fire."[15] For no apparent reason, Lily, taking advantage of her daughter Dina's short absence from Jerusalem, sets out to seduce Dina's fiancé, Yair Yarden. The timing is important: Lily chooses to execute her scheme on the very night she is supposed to meet with Yair's father Yosef to draw up a final list of invitees for Yair and Dina's wedding. The contrapuntal tension between the men's time and the woman's time provides the would-be objective narrator's point of view with an unmistakably ironic edge, for Lily prepares to entrap Yair while he is busy solving a radio quiz show with his younger brother at home. She lures her unsuspecting prey out into the night, while Yosef Yarden and his friend Dr. Kleinberger are playing chess and debating political issues. And while the two men are speculating about the possible causes that might have prevented the reliable and punctilious woman from keeping her appointment, she finally pounces on the helpless victim of her lust.

Having taken Yair for a drink in a local hangout of thugs and bums, Lily tells Yair that she had been married to his father for four months before she married Dina's father. Although she (or the narrator) does not suggest that Dina is therefore Yair's sister, the impact of her story appears to unsettle the young man. Lily takes advantage of his confusion to press forward with her temptation: "No, I am not confused, Yair. I am clearminded and freezing cold. Don't leave me Yair. Touch me, touch me, not like this, not gently, not politely, Yair, not politely, touch hard, hard. I am not fragile, Yair, I am not Dina. I am very sturdy" (1965, p. 172). Lily's clearheadedness emphasizes her moral depravity. Her conduct may have been rather more excusable were she in fact intoxicated or overcome by a sudden outburst of passion, as is Damkov in "Where the Jackals Howl."[16] What further adds to the odiousness of Lily's attraction to Yair is the potentially incestuous element in it, as well as the possibility that her night with Yair may jeopardize her daughter's wedding. Lily's condescending reference to Dina's fragility, however, makes it clear that nothing, not even her maternal responsibility, may hinder her from giving vent to her sexual needs.

It is never too clear what else besides sexual appetite motivates Lily Danenberg. Her nostalgic references to German culture may imply that Lily is trying to unleash her hostility against Israel by avenging herself on the native Israeli couple. But this speculation receives little substantiation from the text. It would seem rather that Lily's national and cultural Otherness serves as an *analogy to*, rather than an explanation of, her moral Otherness. In a similar vein, it is possible to interpret her sadistic treatment of the tomcat on her way to Yair's home as analogous and complementary to her attitude to Yair Yarden. As the animal abandons itself to Lily's explicitly seductive caresses," the divorcee's fists were suddenly raised, formed a bow in the air and struck ferociously at the cat's belly" (1965, p. 156). Lily strikes at the helpless, trusting creature for the same reason she strikes out at Yair, Dina, and Yosef. The reason resides in the dark, libidinal forces that control "the divorcee," who seems to be divorced from humanity and civilization.

The narrative suggests, then, that Lily's sexual appetite is perversely sadistic. It is never too clear whether her sexual behavior is motivated by an unbridled sadistic drive or whether her frustrated sexual needs fuel her ruthlessness. What is clear is that Oz deprives Lily of that mediating mechanism we normally call "conscience." The lack of conscience, the inability to experience moral doubts, conflict, remorse, guilt, or responsibility, is what best typifies Lily as well as Tova, Batya, Galila, and Bruria. Lily's association with the tomcat, Batya's association with the cadavers of flies and insatiable fish, Geula's with a viper, and Galia's with a young jackal suggest a subtle affinity between female sexuality and the anthropocentric vision of animals as purely libidinal creatures. Like the animals with which they are associated, these female protagonists have something in common with their male counterparts, though what they do *not* share with the men—their Otherness—emerges more forcefully.

In Yehoshua's early stories, the female character is an unattainable object of desire who lacks consciousness. Oz's early female characters are voracious sexual creatures who lack conscience. The primacy of the sexual factor in Oz's characterization of women seems to confirm Otto Weininger's conclusion: "The female principle is, then, nothing more than sexuality; the male principle is sexual and something more . . . The sexual instinct is always active in woman . . . whilst in man it is at rest from time to time."[17] The association of woman's allegedly hyperactive "sexual instinct" with moral depravity reflects the male-centered perception of female sexuality as the expression of a fundamental and dangerous Otherness.

Elsewhere Perhaps: Amos Oz's Gyniconology and National Otherness

The title of Amos Oz's first novel, *Maqom Aher* (1966), known to English-speaking readers as *Elsewhere Perhaps*, means literally 'another place.' As such, it alludes to the psychological topography of the novel's major female character, Noga Harish, a native of kibbutz Metzudat Ram, and of her mother Eva, whose longings for another place have caused her to desert her family and elope to post–World War II Germany.

The selection of post-Holocaust Germany as the locus of Eva's longing is not accidental. Like the kibbutz, which often symbolizes a microcosmic, national Self, the symbolic function of Germany in Israeli letters is often associated with national Otherness. The implication of this symbolic polarization is vital to our understanding of Eva's gyniconology as the archetypal Other. It is also possible, however, to read in the title an ironic reference to the idealization of the kibbutz as an/other place, the perfect locus of the idealistic dreams of the early socialist Zionists.

These two readings of the novel's title are closely related, for according to *Elsewhere Perhaps*, the romantic desire for perfection leads—paradoxically—to the abdication of the national homeland. The desire for perfection and its correlate, the impatience with reality, emerges as the fundamental principle of this novel's gyniconologies, or presentations of women. Although some male characters in *Elsewhere Perhaps* are not immune to romantic visions of life or people, they seem somehow to grow out of them. But the novel's mythogynies seem to suggest that the desire for a perfect place is especially typical of women. That this desire is reprehensible is suggested by its association with post–World War II Germany and the threat of abdicating the kibbutz.

The series of misfortunes that befall Reuven Harish, the novel's protagonist, begin with his wife Eva's elopement to Germany with her cousin-turned-lover, Isaac Hamburger. The omniscient though reticent narrator argues that it was Reuven's "purity" that led to his tragedy: "A bright-eyed and pure-hearted lad, what did his pure eyes see, what could they see in Eva? A girl with romantic tendencies . . . His eyes were pure. Could he at all imagine?"[18]

The unfolding plot reveals, however, that when women are involved, a man's "pure eyes" and "pure heart" are grave liabilities. Reuven Harish should have known what his beautiful wife's "romantic tendencies"—her artistic aspirations, her longing for other places, notably European landscapes—might lead to. Reuven Harish, the kibbutz ideologue and educator, knew how to write poems, but was unable to read the obvious connotations of Eva's (Eva's) name. He was not "farsighted" enough to realize that physical beauty, artistic aspirations, and excessive energy in a woman are a lethal combination, or "like seething poison," to use the narrator's words (p. 16). The implied author's tendency to withhold information about or explain Eva's intention to "purify" Hamburger of his suffering (p. 157) appears to confirm the judgments of the narrator, as well as of Reuven, according to whom Eva ran off with "a scumbag," because she was seized by "passion" and "madness" (pp. 156–157). Nevertheless, Reuven is slightly satirized for his naiveté and failure to realize that only mischief could ensue from a young romantic beauty like Eva, who "loves mystery tales and sentimental stories about geniuses afflicted with pneumonia, who expire in their youth" and "frightening Gothic stories about wizards and forests and virgins sacrificing their hymen to the wild storm" (p. 87).

Ironically, it is Reuven's high-minded humanitarianism that leads indirectly to Eva's elopement with Hamburger, for it is at his behest that she is reconciled with the cousin she used to despise. There is a faint allusion in the text to Eva's desire to "purify" the manipulative and licentious businessman, but since no details are provided about the meaning or manner of this "purification," one is left to deduce that Eva is merely rationalizing a self-destructive urge to join her evil cousin and abandon her good husband. The narrator does not emphasize Eva's materialistic proclivities, but he does allude to the material aspect of Eva's attraction for Germany, in addition to her romantic susceptibility to Gothic romance and landscape. Eva's return to Germany suggests that she is returning in more than one way to the upper-middle-class life-style of which her mother Stella was so proud. By leaving the kibbutz, Eva is belatedly accepting Stella's opposition to Israel and to Reuven Harish. By preferring the slimy Hamburger, whose "diasporic" name evokes not only the name of the German city of Hamburg, but also a fast food product, to Harish, whose Hebrew name means 'ploughing', Eva enacts a literal and symbolic betrayal of socialist Zionism.

Eva rationalizes her abdication of the kibbutz and her family by claiming that she wishes to purify her cousin. The fallacy of her thinking evokes ever so subtly non-Zionist philosophies concerning the presumed role of the dispersion of Jews in the world. Eva's mythogyny may also be read as an indictment of Jewish immigrants who returned to the Diaspora under some false pretext. Her desire for the other place is in some important ways more reprehensible than Hamburger's, who never experienced life in the kibbutz.[19]

Left alone with Noga and Guy, his two young children, Reuven Harish tries to survive his wife's elopement. Always the high-minded humanitarian, he refrains from criticizing their mother's move. But, as the narrator puts it, apparently somewhat critical of Reuven's self-justification, "a man in his prime and in his best years cannot live long without a woman" (p. 20). This explains why Reuven failed to reject Bronka Berger, his friend's middle-aged wife, when ten months after Eva's departure she "found her way to Reuven Harish's bed" (p. 21). The narrator makes it clear that Reuven did not initiate the affair, that he "did not try to court or seduce her," and that Bronka "hinted" that she would consent, "of her own will" (p. 55). Yet Reuven will pay dearly for his second failure to avoid the wrong woman. For one thing, Reuven is afflicted with moral compunctions and guilt. Bronka Berger, on the other hand, is never shown to share such feelings, apparently because she seems so preoccupied with her body: "Bronka thinks of her body. With slight disgust she thinks of her body . . . They say that getting old is particularly rough on women who used to be beautiful. I was not beautiful" (p. 52).[20]

Reuven's affair with Bronka paves the way to his most lethal entanglement with a woman, his own daughter, Noga. For by becoming involved with Bronka Berger, Reuven loses the moral authority with which he might have dissuaded Noga from carrying on an affair with Bronka's husband and his own good friend, Ezra Berger. Reuven's physical deterioration, which begins with his wife's desertion, is exacerbated by Noga's affair with Ezra. His already fragile state of health worsens when

Noga refuses to undergo an abortion. When Reuven finds out, toward the end of the novel, that Ezra's brother and Hamburger's business mate, Siegfried Berger, came to the kibbutz to lure Noga to join Eva in Germany, he is overcome by a fatal heart attack.

Reuven Harish is gradually undermined by women. It is no coincidence that his heart—the symbolic locus of his love for Eva and Noga—is his weak point. Yet the physical deterioration of Reuven Harish is accompanied by a process of spiritual growth. As he develops from a naive, self-deluding idealist into a tolerant and somewhat disillusioned realist, the implied author's ironic distance is gradually modified. Although he does not cut as admirable a figure as his double, Herbert Segal, Reuven nevertheless emerges at the end as a sympathetic, even somewhat tragic, character.[21]

The opposite process appears to underlie the gyniconology of Noga, the novel's central female character. Presented first as a charming and vivacious young girl, Noga appears to embody what her name (which means both 'light' and 'Venus') denotes. Gradually, however, her nickname, Stella—the name of her evil grandmother—constitutes an equally important aspect of her character (pp. 34–35). Like her beautiful mother, Noga combines hedonism and a romantic kind of spirituality. She dreams about "other" places and is fascinated by immoral or antisocial behavior (as in her affair with Ezra Berger) and by wayward foreigners (as in her relationship with Zecharia Berger). Like her mother, she tends to rationalize her unseemly conduct in lofty romantic terms which make little sense (she believes her affair with Ezra will "purify" him). Although her additional nickname, Turkisa, alludes to her indebtedness to both her green-eyed father and her blue-eyed mother, an allusion we may interpret as her simultaneous attraction to Eva's libido and Reuven's scruples, it appears that Eva has the upper hand. For like her mother, Noga rejects a man who loves her—the good-looking idealistic Rami Rimmon—and prefers to carry on a scandalous affair with Ezra, a married soon-to-be grandfather. Like her mother, Noga is not mindful of Reuven Harish or the kibbutz in general, and like her she prefers cheap thrills to a man's true love.

While I agree with Nurith Gertz's reading of the shift in the narrator's distance from Reuven Harish, I do not agree with her thesis that the narrator confirms that "Noga is deserving of love," as she puts it.[22] In my opinion, the narrator uses the wrongheaded judgment of the naive members of the kibbutz as an ironic ploy. The narrator is poking fun at the tendency of the members to interpret Noga's attractiveness as her inner strength. For one thing, the members do not know that it was Noga who seduced Ezra Berger. The following excerpt dramatizes the irresistibility of Noga's seductive ploys, implicitly justifying Berger's publicly condemned behavior: "She presses her body to the metal door [of Ezra's truck] and sends a coaxing smile to the man's face . . . Noga's legs are restless . . . 'Ezra, be nice'. Her voice is turning into a whisper . . . The girl put two dark fingers in his sweaty, hairy palm and stated: 'You're sweet' " (pp. 30–31). Noga's seduction of Berger is to some extent reminiscent of Galila's interest in Damkov's grotesquely virile body. It is possible to interpret the alleged attraction of teenage beauties to older men as the result of an androcentric phantasy. The gyniconologies of Noga and Galila reify conventional androcentric preferences in much the same way that the self-loathing of Batya Pinsky and Bronka Berger do.

The scene in which Turkisa asks Ezra to buy her a spool of turquoise thread is the first in a series of seductive traps which will ultimately ensnare the virile cynic in the nymphet's net. Noga's flirtatious maneuvers culminate in her attempt to practically force Ezra to have intercourse with her. While Noga "fights" and "refuses to let go of him," Ezra tries in vain to dissuade her: "But you are ill, you are feverish, go to bed, my child. Your whole body is trembling. Did you go mad?" (p. 159). But the teenage virgin is unyielding, while the "exhausted" and "confused" experienced man is trying to beat an unsuccessful retreat: "The man tries to push her away, [but] she clings to his clothes with her nails. [He feels] her soft kisses on his hairy and sweaty chest. Backwards, backwards she drags him, with her small steps, into the depth of the myrtle bushes, into the dark thicket . . . Overcome, he falls over with his heavy palms on her shoulders" (p. 159). The description of Noga's successful seduction of Ezra (note the perennial evocation of a gardenlike context as the scene of temptations) implies that the daughter not only mimics but outdoes her mother. For while Eva *follows* Hamburger, Noga "drags" Ezra "backward," both literally and figuratively.

Noga's seductive ploys can only be compared to the maneuvers she undertakes during her first sexual encounter with Berger. The inexperienced virgin overwhelms the man, who unwillingly succumbs to her irresistible powers: "Who taught her tongue to caress like this, with gentle licks, his salty neck? Whence her fingers' wisdom at his nape?" (p. 159). Noga's sexual know-how can only rival her ability to reach multiple orgasm during her first intercourse, though both are in a sense outdone by the versatility of the water imagery Oz employs in this scene. The "ripples," "flooding torrents," "wave after wave," "whirls," "boiling water," "streaming jet," and "roaring waterfalls" are almost taken for granted by both Noga and Ezra as the natural sequel to a girl's first sexual experience. The answer to the explicit and implicit questions about Noga's sexual virtuosity is offered in the chapter's title "A Woman." Being a woman, Noga does not have to be "taught" how to "caress," "lick," or use her fingers wisely. Being a woman, Noga does not require the maturity and experience that men do. Since sexual prowess is synonymous with female nature, Noga is beyond (or below?) the human trajectory from innocence to experience. Noga is experienced because no woman is ever innocent or inexperienced—it is against her nature to be so.[23]

But why does Noga seduce Ezra Berger? Since it is clear that she is not in love with him, the most obvious explanations for her conduct are her marked resemblance to her mother and her unbridled sexuality. Like her licentious mother, Noga is incapable of rational or moral thinking: "Turkisa does not think of things but of shapes. She thinks of light embroideries covered with delicate patterns that cannot be materialized in concrete reality. Noga does not like concrete reality because it is coarse. Even without knowing her well, you can see she has dreams" (p. 199). Noga's mind appears to produce images rather than thoughts. Her preference for "delicate patterns that cannot be materialized in reality" and her revulsion from "concrete reality" (p. 199) are consonant with her mother's romantic longings for other places. Her susceptibility to dreams, her tendency to identify with fictional characters, and her search for "a crack in a legend through which to enter" (p. 201) are reminiscent of her mother's attraction to Gothic romances. One of Noga's dreams is "to travel one day to a land of murderers and see" (p. 201), which is precisely what Eva ends up doing. This attraction to "a land of murderers" suggests that Noga lacks the fundamental moral capacity to prefer right to wrong. The lack of conscience explains her willingness to carry on an affair with Berger (without much loving him) as well as her inability to have doubts or to feel remorse.

Noga's internal monologues also reveal an infantile and crude form of narcissism, which may explain her indifference to, or unawareness of, the anguish she inflicts on both Rami and Reuven: "They both [Rami and Ezra] love me and I also love me and I also love that they love me because I love to be loved" (p. 199). Whereas Ezra is deeply disturbed by his affair with Noga (although he has his own axe to grind), Noga appears to be blithely free of any regrets. She is too smug to notice Rami's despair, Ezra's doubts, and the devastating impact of her affair on Reuven. Noga's smugness complements a nearly megalomaniacal sense of superiority. "She likes to think of herself as chosen to be a clapper of a bell . . . She is always the clapper of the world" (p. 200). The image of the clapper of the bell suggests that behind Noga's scandalous behavior lies a desire to be noticed by everybody.

Noga's infantile rationalizations further undermine the validity of her point of view. Like Eva, Noga believes that she must "purify" what she perceives as a suffering man by becoming involved with him. The following internal monologue exemplifies her irrational thinking: "Now Ezra, listen up: you must remember one thing. I love a horse because it is wild and I must purify [you] because I am responsible [for you]" (p. 158). The paratactic logic (or rather illogic) of Noga's utterances creates a distance between Noga's self-understanding and the implied reader. The run-on sentences and free association typifying her internal monologues undercut her self-justifications and point out the faulty reasoning of her "feminine" mind.[24]

Noga's interpretations of the concepts of purification and responsibility are also laughable because in "actuality" she makes a travesty of both. In addition to the incongruity between her actions and her view of herself, the implied author uses a set of internal contradictions as a primary means of ironic self-betrayal. For example, Noga believes at one point that she is purifying Ezra of his suffering, her implicit premise being that suffering and pain are contaminating or impure. Yet, when pressured to undergo an abortion, Noga insists that she must have the baby because "suffering will purify her" (p. 280).

But if Noga's explanations are suspect, how else are we to interpret her motivations? A subtle reference to what may be lurking beneath Noga's disarmingly innocent surface appears in her response to her father's plea for her to be good: "You always, always, always want everything to always be good. Why should things be good? Why? Why shouldn't they be bad? Why? Yes—bad. When things get worse, they become more real. I tell you, things will then become more alive" (p. 280). This dialogue with her aged and ailing father reveals for the first time that Noga is faintly aware that her behavior is "bad." Furthermore, it alludes to the fact that, in the final analysis, Noga breaks the rules because, to her, evil is more "real" and "alive."

This preference may explain why, while still pregnant with Ezra's baby, Noga begins to consort with the insidious Siegfried (Zecharia) Berger, to the dismay of the entire kibbutz. One may assume that Noga fails to understand the schemes of Siegfried, who is luring her to join her mother in Germany. Noga is fascinated by Siegfried's descriptions of Germany as a land of "forests and lakes, . . . and green dreamy hills" (p. 283). The narrator lets us speculate that naiveté rather than malice motivates Noga at this point. Either way, only her father's death, it would seem, could ever bring an end to her increasingly outrageous conduct. Noga's subsequent rejection of Siegfried and marriage to Rami Rimmon suggest that Reuven Harish had to pay with his life for his daughter's realization that evil makes things neither more real nor more alive. Only her father's death could apparently bring the daughter around to his point of view.

Yet the abrupt transition from the detailed descriptions of Noga's waywardness to the short idyllic scene which ends the novel interferes with the obvious implications of the happy end. The domestic bliss which joins Rami Rimmon, the pregnant Noga, and the Bergers is too perfect. "The Last Scene," which is the title of the last chapter, suggests that the final scene is only a spurious closure. The storm raging outside the quiet and warm room at the Bergers's home suggests that perhaps what we are witnessing is a quiet prelude to yet another storm. The name of Noga's newborn daughter, Inbal (which means a clapper of a bell), intimates that Noga may not have altogether given up her phantasies of herself as the "clapper of the world." We cannot help wondering how soon it will be before Noga abandons once again her father's ways to return to her mother's ways—and ultimately to her true female nature.

To some extent, the implicit explanations for Noga's behavior are tautological. Noga is attracted to the wrong people because of her mother, while her mother does so because she is a woman. By avoiding circumstantial specificities, Oz falls back in his mythogynies on conventional Western thinking regarding the female nature. Female characters have been so often portrayed as wayward and incomprehensible that one is exempt from explaining their motivations. In the words of a rather notorious misogynist: "The well-known phrase, 'women have no character' really means the same thing. Personality and individuality (intelligible), ego and soul, will and (intelligible) character, all these are different expressions of the same actuality, an actuality the male of mankind attains, the female lacks."[25] Is it possible to assume that woman's alleged lack of conscience, or what Weininger would call "intelligible character," accounts for the peculiarities of Amos Oz's gyniconologies?

Joanna Russ has suggested that simplistic and reductive gyniconologies stem from the Western vision of woman as Other: "There is no explanation in terms of human motivation on the woman's own inner life; she simply behaves the way she does because she is a bitch. No other ever has the motives that you and I have; the other contains a mysterious essence which causes it to behave as it does; in fact "it" is not a person at all but a projected wish or fear."[26] The female Other is a convenient locus for the projection of androcentric fears and desires. It is possible to assume that while Noga's irresistible beauty and desire for older men may be understood as the product of male fantasy, the destructive results of her feminine seductiveness embody male fear of female desirability.

Elsewhere Perhaps has often been taken as a national allegory. In this context, the psychological gaps and the implausibility of Noga's characterization may not be as disturbing. As the daughter of Reuven Harish, the high-minded idealist, and of Eva Harish, the spoiled, middle-class romantic, Noga may represent the state of Israel, which has to choose between the legacy of socialist Zionist ideals and European bourgeois compromises. Nurith Gertz is right in pointing out the negative impact that the compensation agreement with Germany (1953) and the Sinai War (1956) had on the state's elite.[27] We might speculate, then, that Oz's mythogynies in *Elsewhere Perhaps* encode a political critique of the adolescent state and its disappointing policies. By underscoring the irreconcilable combination in Noga of her desire to put an end to Ezra's (or Siegfried's) suffering and her tendency to torture her father, Oz may be alluding to the state's professed intention to put an end to Jewish suffering while prolonging it by becoming embroiled in unnecessary wars.

My Michael: Woman as Political Enemy

My Michael (1968) is Oz's first and thus far most consistent effort to present an Israeli woman's world from "her own" point of view. As the protagonist and first-person narrator of the novel, Hana Gonen seems not only to have the final word on the presentation and judgment of the novel's characters and events, but also to give expression to the implied narrator's point of view. In an article about his creative writing, Oz affirms that Hana is not an artistic illusion but a "real" character, and in many ways the novel's author:

> Michael's Hana, for example, insisted, nagged me for a long time. She did not give up. She said to me: 'Look, I am here, I will not let you go. You will write what I am telling you [to write], or you will have no peace. And I argued back, I excused myself; I told her: Look, I cannot [do it], go to somebody else. Go to some woman author; I am not a woman; I cannot write you in the first person; leave me alone. But no, she did not give up. And then, when I wrote, to get rid of her, and return somehow to my own life, she nevertheless continued to argue

about every line, day and night. She wanted me to write in a certain
way, and to expand the story. I said that was impossible, bad, ex-
traneous, [I said] it was my novel—not hers, and that after all she was
my *dybbuk* and not the other way around.[28]

In this endearingly playful expansion of the romantic idea that the
artist is the slave of his creation, Oz is playfully justifying not only his use
of a female protagonist-narrator, but also the novel's omissions, repeti-
tions and excesses. By disclaiming responsibility for his mythogynous
creation, and attributing it to his heroine he is claiming authenticity and
legitimacy for his interpretation (invention?) of womanhood. By presenting himself as a mere medium of a powerful female *dybbuk*, Oz is asking
us to regard his maleness as incidental or irrelevant to his creation. For,
after all, it was Hana, who, refusing to resort to a female author, forced
her story on him. As we shall see, however, Hana Gonen is more like a
voodoo doll, than a tyrannical *dybbuk*. The pins Oz sticks into
his gyniconological creation subtly invalidate Hana's point of view.[29]
The implied author entraps the heroine by planting belief system
and by constructing multiple sets of incongruities between what
emerges as the referential reality and Hana's interpretation of it.

For example, though the implied reader is first coaxed into adopting
Hana's disparaging view of her uninspiring husband Michael and is lured
into sympathizing with her plight, it soon becomes clear that this plight
is a false projection of Hana's self-pity. By denying Hana's constraints and
insisting on Michael's devotion to her, the implied author suggests that
the heroine is the victim of her own romantic dreams. In many ways, Oz
is undercutting the tragic or heroic protagonist of the conventional
European female-centered novel.[30] He does it mainly by depriving Hana
of real problems. Hana does not have to earn a living because Michael
supports her. She does not have to exert herself too much in raising her
son because Michael takes care of him. Since Michael provides her with a
maid when he becomes too busy to take upon himself the household
chores, she is released from that burden. Her problems are mainly
caused by herself. She isolates herself from friends and family, and later
does all she can to make herself sick. Her real problem, it would seem,
stems from her unrealistic expectations from life. She suffers from a
hyperactive imagination and an inability to separate fiction from reality.
To a large extent, she does not differ from Noga and Eva, who expect
reality to conform to their infantile dreams. Yet Oz's version of Madame
Bovary differs from that of his previous heroines to the extent that Hana

lets her dreams control her life and hurt Michael, her husband, and Yair, her first-born son.

The opening sentences of *My Michael* present what might be regarded as Hana's most significant self-delusion: "I am writing because people that I used to love, already died. I am writing because when I was a child I had much strength to love and now my strength to love is going to die. I do not want to die."[31] The unfolding plot invalidates Hana's opening statement. Her father, now dead, is one of the people Hana supposedly loved. Yet her more detailed references to him express condescension intermingled with pity: "I remember him thus: standing and washing dishes in my mother's apron . . . He would respect the opinion of every nincompoop, obliged to ingratiate himself, as if every person had the power to judge him" (p. 23). Yehezkel, Michael's father, who also dies in the course of the story, may not have inspired Hana's anger and revulsion, as did Michael's aunts, but neither is there any evidence that she loved him. It is clear that she cannot bear her mother and despises her brother Emanuel. She mentions favorably her friend Hadassa, but nothing seems to demonstrate that she had anything for her that might even remotely be interpreted as love. It is rather clear that she hates Yardena, Michael's colleague, and shows no interest in any of his other friends. Just as she was indifferent if not outright hostile towards Mrs. Tarnopoler, her old landlady, and Mrs. Sara Zeldin, in whose kindergarten she used to work before her marriage, she is bored and annoyed by her neighbors the Glicks and Mr. Kadishman. As to her strength to love as a child, the only childhood playmates she constantly refers to throughout the novel, the Palestinian twins Halil and Aziz, emerge rather as servants than as truly beloved friends. And just as she enjoyed her superiority over the twins, she is trying to turn the naive, orthodox teenager, Yoram Kaminitzer, who is helplessly ensnared by her charms, into her slave: "He was in my hands. I ruled him. All of him. I could paint on his face any expression I desired. Like on a piece of paper. Many years have passed since I last enjoyed this kind of cold game" (p. 161). Through Yoram Kaminitzer, Hana hopes to recreate her real or imagined relationship with Halil and Aziz and to realize her fantasy about her childhood hero Michael Strogoff, "to subject for the last time a last Michael Strogoff to the discipline and mission of a demoted princess" (p. 162). Thus the novel belies Hana's self-perception by demonstrating that she never loved anyone, as well as by alluding to the fact that what she interprets as love is nothing but a power game between victim and victor.

Hana is incapable of feeling love even for her own son. When Yair is born, Hana becomes sick, letting the hardworking Michael take care of the baby until she recovers. That Hana's sickness is an excuse or a physical manifestation of her psychological rejection of her son becomes clear when Hana becomes well again. For although she is able to take care of the baby, she tends to neglect him. Hana's sickness (she becomes sick again when she gives birth to a second baby at the end of the novel) may also be interpreted as a metaphorical expression for her mental sickness—namely, her maternal dysfunctioning. Shortly after Yair's birth, she tells her stupefied husband that she believes her son will not grow into an intelligent man. She never plays with the child, but lets Michael teach him how to speak, take his first steps, and later read and solve sophisticated riddles. Instead of sharing a dentist's admiration for her son's mature attitude, she is "disgusted" by it. "A five-year-old child who is exuberant over dental disease will grow up and become a repulsive man" (p. 161). Hana's hostility towards Yair reaches its climax when she believes she has diagnosed in him a virile self-control, which she perceives as prideful defiance: "I would beat Yair whenever he showed his sullen pride. Panting, avoiding his calm gray eyes I would thrash him, until I managed to wrest the sobbing from his throat" (p. 82). In other words, Hana acts out her obsession with, and envy of, male power even in the unlikely context of a mother-child relationship. By beating up her son, she hopes to undermine his budding masculinity and to reduce him to a whimpering, helpless child over whom she can exercise her authority more successfully. Outraged by Yair's emotional maturity, Hana reveals not only a bad case of penis envy but her own infantile nature. For it is she rather than Yair who throws tantrums and pretends to be sick to shirk her responsibilities. And it is she who molds her expectations on fairy tales and childrens' stories. Like Ruth Kipnis, her counterpart in "The Hill of Evil Counsel" (1976), it is she who emerges as the true child in relation to her son.[32]

From a connotational viewpoint, Hana can be seen as an Israeli version of the castrating mother. It has been noted that whereas the incrimination of wives is a common theme in different national literatures of all ages, twentieth century Western fiction is especially acrimonious in its critique of women as mothers.[33] Katherine Rogers explains this literary tendency as a backlash against the legal rights granted to Western women early in the twentieth century. It is also possible to explain the backlash against mothers as a result of the popularization of Freudian theories about early infancy. On the other hand, recent sociological and psychoanalytic studies suggest that the literary portrayals of castrating mothers express what Dorothy Dinnerstein calls "the human malaise" produced by the restrictive attribution of parenting to mothers.[34]

But Hana's maternal dysfunctioning is, as already noted, only one manifestation of her inability to love, or rather her perverse tendency to translate love into power. The most odious results of this fundamental flaw find expression in Hana's attitude to Michael. Although she claims that she "loved him" (p. 5), there is little in the novel to bear it out. Even before their marriage, Hana often feels estranged from Michael. The austere solemnity of the wedding ceremony itself is evocative of a funeral march (p. 37). Hana's ironic presentation of Michael as a conventional, unimaginative companion lures us first to sympathize with her dismissive attitude towards him. As the novel progresses, however, it becomes clear that, for all her glamorous self-image, Hana is little more than the typical frustrated homemaker. Her own thinking betrays her dependence on middle-class convention. Instead of making demands on herself, she criticizes her husband for his failure to live up to her romantic expectations and indulges herself with shopping sprees and daydreams.

Oblivious (or indifferent?) to Michael's desperate efforts to make ends meet, Hana gives vent to her materialistic appetites during especially stressful times. Nevertheless, she remains dissatisfied when Michael takes on additional work and so succeeds in giving her all the conveniences she has demanded: a telephone, a maid, and finally a private home. Unable (or unwilling) to persevere with any job, Hana gives up her position as a kindergarten teacher and later her part-time job as a clerk, as well as her interest in the university courses she had been auditing before her marriage. While she abandons herself to real or imagined sicknesses, Michael perseveres with his career, progressing from his B.A. to a Ph.D. in Geology, and earns a position as a university lecturer. Michael's achievements in no way mitigate Hana's condescending view of her husband: "You were born and you will die in the shape of a miserable zero, Michael Ganz. Period." (p. 179).

Hana's demands for Michael's attention and services during the most trying periods in his career (during his crucial final examinations, Michael is required to take care of his sick wife and new-born baby), as well as the timing of her extravagant shopping sprees, suggest that Hana is not merely a disgruntled housewife disappointed with her husband's failure to match the legendary Michael Strogoff, her childhood hero and knight in shining armor. These actions, combined with her nagging complaints and sarcastic remarks, suggest that Hana is making an attempt to undermine her husband. Infuriated by her husband's self-control, tolerance, and patience, she does all she can to shatter his composure. The reason for this attempt may be construed from her relationships with other men: her desire to dominate or be dominated by them. She argues that she "did not ask for a wild man" (p. 40), yet all her erotic dreams, as we shall see, revolve around violent brutes or obedient slaves. Michael's virile self-control, on the one hand, and his sensitive gentleness, on the other, are the wrong response to Hana's sadomasochistic needs, for they are in essence expressions of love, not of power.

Towards the end of the novel, as Hana's self-destructive actions become more obvious, her attempt to undermine her husband also emerges with unprecedented clarity. Vaguely cognizant of her failure to destroy Michael, she tries one last ploy: "I used to wake up my husband, creeping underneath his blanket. I fastened myself to his body with all my might, squeezing and squeezing out of his body the desirable self-control . . . Yet, I ignored him. I related to his body only: muscles, arms, hair. In my heart I knew that I betrayed him over and over again with his own body" (p. 178). Oz is offering us a reversal of the literary convention of the betrayed and abandoned heroine. Here the husband is presented as the tragic victim of nymphomaniacal callousness. Yet Oz remains loyal to the moralistic denouement of the romantic plot. The heartless abuser—here the woman—is punished through her own actions. Her erratic conduct ends up by alienating Michael, who toward the end of the novel begins for the first time to abandon her. Worse, Hana becomes gradually alienated from reality, and towards the end of the novel we realize that she is well on the way to clinical insanity.

The image of the desirable, castrating wife can be seen as a modern version of the gynophobic portrayals of Delilah and Jezebel, the Sirens, and the Lorelei. Karen Horney says in this connection that male-authored portrayals of dangerous yet desirable women are an attempt to validate a male sexual fear of women: " 'It is not', he [man] says, 'that I dread her, it is that she herself is malignant, capable of any crime, a beast of prey, a vampire, a witch, insatiable in her desires. She is the very personification of what is sinister.' "[35] Oz's gyniconology reiterates this kind of androcentric thinking. By resorting to the personal subjective point of view and the narrated monologue, by letting Hana speak for herself, as it were, Oz seems to declare that it is not male-produced mythogynies, but the nature of woman herself, that is the source of trouble in the family, society, and the world.

Hana's fantasies show that the romantic gyniconological polarization of woman on the pedestal and woman as victim reflects woman's innermost wishes. In her fantasy world, Hana thinks she is a princess with the power to subjugate powerful men to her will. In her day-to-day life, she thinks of herself as a victimized woman, deprived of what she deserves. The distinction between dream and reality, however, is a flimsy one, for we often observe Hana ordering her husband about and virtually torturing her son. Hana's fantasies, which appear with increasing frequency as the novel progresses, reveal that her inner world is informed by images of violence. In the following excerpt, Hana has a rape fantasy.

Palms were pressing against my body. They were kneading, beating, searching. I laughed and screamed with all my might . . . I am of ice, my city is of ice, and of ice will be the subjects. All of them. The princess proclaimed a law. Hail will come upon Danzig, and will beat down the entire city, crystal clear, transparent and forceful. Down, rebellious subjects, down. Beat [your] brows against the snow" (p. 136).

An interfusion of "hot" and "cold" imagery (a burning wave, men's sweat, snow, hail) and images of brightness and darkness (white plains, stars, fog, darkness) complement the implied incongruity between Hana's national identity and her hidden desire for an association with the German city of Danzig and with Palestinian terrorists. While the combination of what are commonly thought to be opposites may signal the confusion, fluidity, and formlessness of a mind on the verge of a mental breakdown, Hana's secret yearning to be raped also alludes to her sadomasochistic proclivities. Two mythogynies are combined in the above paragraph: woman's susceptibility to madness, and woman's secret desire to be abused.[36]

This fantasy corroborates what Hana's general conduct suggests: that she seeks and enjoys physical disease. She says, "I had fond memories of the diphtheria I had contracted when I was a nine-year-old child" (p. 134). As a mature woman, Hana welcomes her severe cold: "I could not swallow. A burn was scalding my throat. It was a new pain. The more it increased the happier I was" (p. 135). Against the explicit advice of Michael to keep warm, Hana jumps off the bed as soon as he leaves home to take an ice-cold shower: "I opened all the faucets all the way. I wallowed in the ice-cold water . . . My skin grew blue with cold. The warm pain penetrated through my nape, dripping along my spine. The nipples hardened. My toes were petrified. Only my head burned" (p. 136).[37] This attempt to exacerbate her sickness precedes the above-quoted fantasy. The proximity of these descriptions—that of Hana's physical sickness and that of her sadomasochistic fantasy—not only explains the fantasy's contrastive imagery; on a deeper level, it suggests a mutual complementarity. Hana's sadomasochistic fantasy is both the product and a form of a sickness, just as her physical sickness is the product and external manifestation of her sick fantasy life.

As Hana's fantasies grow wilder, her physical illnesses become more frequent. The association of sick body and infected mind persists throughout the novel. The frequent references to sickness suggest that there is nothing ennobling or inspiring about Hana's degeneration into hysteria and psychosis. In the absence of any specific reasons (such as childhood traumas or genetic disorder), we must assume that the author is relying for credibility on the common association, especially in

Western literature, between madness and femaleness. As Vivian Gornick puts it, woman is "most female when she goes mad."[38] Hana's madness is the logical culmination of her actions, or rather nonactions, throughout the novel. Her refusal to take upon herself any kind of responsibility, her hostility towards her husband and son, and her indifference to her social and national milieu are explained as symptoms of an innate mental disease. From this point of view, Hana represents the typical male-created madwoman. As Mary Allen puts it: "When woman goes mad . . . she is distinctly at odds with her society, but not in a way either attractive or acceptable to the reader. Her breakdown is a shattering that reveals the ugliness, not the imagination, of her inner being. Referring to a hero as a madman is not at all like calling a heroine crazy."[39] And indeed, Hana's mental degeneration, which becomes especially exacerbated towards the end of the novel, reveals "the ugliness, not the imagination, of her inner being." It might have been different if she had been presented as the victim of an oppressive marriage or of social and economic constraints. As we have seen, however, this is not the case. Since Hana is the only cause for her misery, there is no escaping the conclusion that her mental breakdown is not an aberration, not a deviation, from her innermost being, but rather the necessary product of an inherent malignancy.

That this malignancy is vitally connected with her femaleness is demonstrated both by the fact that no other reasons are enlisted to explain her degeneration, and also by the other female characters in the novel. Thus, for example, the childless, loud, and dominant aunt Genia, a chain-smoking, vulgar pediatrician whose constant meddling in the couple's life is gratuitous and annoying, turns toward the end of the novel into a caricature of the "manly woman," the power-crazed, neurotic, professional woman: "Her voice became thick and heavy. When she lit a cigarette, she used to curse herself in Polish . . . Aunt Genia's hair grew thin and gray. Her face began to resemble the face of an old malicious man" (p. 177). At the same time, the childless, middle-aged Duba Glick, Hana's next-door neighbor, is a caricature of the passive, confined, mad housewife. Mrs. Glick's increasingly hysterical and violent fits of paranoia (she believes herself to be persecuted by the neighborhood's children) force her gentle and tolerant husband to commit her to a mental asylum, from which she is later to emerge debilitated, old, and fat. Like Hana Gonen, both Aunt Genia and Mrs. Glick degenerate by varying degrees into physical and mental disease. In the absence of even one healthy female character, one is tempted to conclude that femininity itself is a kind of psychosomatic disease, whose damning results are unavoidable.

This conclusion is almost inescapable given the absence of sufficient reasons for Hana's degeneration. What we have instead are few and cryptic references to general truisms which might be applied to Hana's case. For example, early in the novel, Michael says to Hana, "Emotion swells and becomes a malignant growth when people are satiated and have too much leisure time" (p. 20). At this point we might be tempted to dismiss Michael's observation as "banal", as Hana does. Yet toward the end of the novel her emotional malignancy is exacerbated by her leisure time and middle-class comfort. There are also a few subtle archetypal references to the female nature that might be construed as explanations for Hana's demise. For example, Hana's dialogue with the hopelessly enamored Yoram is punctuated by Yair's apparently innocent questions about snakes' cold blood (p. 160). Yair's questions are *prima facie* childish importunities, but they may also be construed as a subtle evocation of Hana's ruthlessness and a reptile's cold blood, or of the primeval association of Eve and the serpent.

But to say that Hana is evil because she is the daughter of Eve is to use circular reasoning that seeks to prove what it takes for granted. It is just like arguing that she is immoral because she is mad, mad because she is sick, and sick because she is a woman. The underlying premise in this circular reasoning is that woman is an Other who is different and inferior to man. Gershon Shaked argues that Oz's characters should be understood as archetypal manifestations of forces residing in every human psyche.[40] The problem with such an explanation is that by resorting to Jungian concepts, it tries to dignify what are nothing more than conventional, androcentric mythogynies. For one thing, Oz does not rely on archetypal forces to explain the motivations of Michael. We learn more about Michael's past and family than about Hana's. It therefore makes no sense to justify Oz's problematic gyniconology by resorting to the novel's allegedly metarealistic character.

I would like to suggest that the reasons for the widely shared acceptance of Oz's gyniconologies as verisimilar or plausible have to do with what Gérard Genette calls an "approved maxim": "To understand the behavior of a character (for example), is to be able to refer it back to an approved maxim, and this reference is perceived as a demonstration of cause and effect."[41]

Hence it is possible that the contrast between Michael's emotional and professional growth and Hana's degeneration derives its plausibility from widely shared maxims. It is possible that critics have thus far not challenged the characterizations of Hana and Michael because they are no less vulnerable to these entrenched maxims than authors.

In this context, it is worthwhile to mention Elizabeth Ermarth's argument that fictional consensus, which is often identified with verisimilitude or realism in the traditional novel, applies differently to male and female characters.[42] Ermarth notes that while the conflict between the individual and the community is a common theme in traditional realistic fiction, there is a considerably higher proportion "of important female casualties." As she says, "the conflict proves fatal to a surprising number of heroines" (p. 10). Hana Gonen seems to belong to a large group of heroines doomed for their anti-social tendencies. Madness, illness or death are common resolutions for "deviant" heroines in the androcentric realistic novel. As Ermarth puts it: "For the heroine's progress is converted into a slow attrition which kills her. She experiences not time for growth but time running out" (p. 2).

Hana Gonen's fundamental conflict with her society ends with her defeat. Her refusal to accept her prescribed role as a good mother and wife sets in motion the inevitable process of her degeneration. Her attempt to break out of this role is condemned as vainglorious and destructive. Her indifference to her husband and son prove to be just as wrongheaded as Eva Harish's desertion of her family. Perhaps the most significant difference between Eva and Hana is that Hana does not succeed in undermining her husband and son. Like Hans Kipnis and Hillel in "The Hill of Evil Counsel" (1976), Michael and Yair emerge relatively unscathed from their confrontation with their mad wife and mother.[43] It is Hana herself who is the primary victim of her misguided actions and sick delusions.

Summary

Joanna Russ's summary of the typical androcentric mythogyny fits Amos Oz's heroines very well. According to Russ, the traditional male-created heroine is restricted to "one vice, one virtue and one occupation . . . How she got married, how she did not get married (tragic). How she fell in love and committed adultery, how she saved her marriage but just barely. How she loved a vile seducer and eloped or eloped and died at childbirth. How she went mad."[44]

There is, however, a unique aspect in Oz's gyniconology that reflects a specifically Israeli set of anxieties and preoccupations. His heroines are not merely Others in the psychological or moral sense, but also in the political sense. They are not merely the traitors of their husbands and children; they also betray their country. Since in Oz's fiction, male characters are for the most part spokesmen of the national Self, it is not difficult to understand the high correlation between a woman's imagined or actual adultery and her betrayal of Israel or the fundamental principles of socialist Zionism. Lily Danenberg despises the Hebrew language and longs for her native Germany, while Geula craves to have intercourse with a Bedouin pilferer who encroaches on her kibbutz's preserves. Noga Harish dreams about escaping to post–World War II Germany, to where her mother Eva immigrated from the kibbutz. In "The Hill of Evil Counsel," Ruth Kipnis deserts Jerusalem in the company of a licentious British admiral—the unmistakable symbol of the oppressive regime of the British Mandate. Ruth feels just as alienated in Jerusalem as the snobbish lady Bromely, who sees Jerusalem as "a despicable hole" and a "vulgar parody" (p. 51). The Russian-born Lyubov Binyamina also grows tired of the Jewish state and ends up immigrating to her sister in the United States, where "she was run over, or perhaps threw herself under a train" (p. 54).

Perhaps the most blatant portrayal of an Israeli woman as a national traitor is Hana Gonen. When Michael is drafted for the Sinai War, Hana spends her days in bed, having orgiastic fantasies about Palestinian terrorists. The violence of her dreams is one characteristic which would seem to forestall a sympathetic interpretation of her indifference to the war (as, for example, an expression of pacifism). At the end of the novel, Hana visualizes herself dispatching Halil and Aziz on a terrorist mission whose goal is to explode the central water supply of Jerusalem: "I will set them on. By evening both will crouch to prepare their supplies for the journey: faded military backpacks, a box of explosives, detonators, fuses, ammunition, handgrenades, glittering knives" (pp. 196–197).

It is possible to interpret Hana Gonen as a symbolic representation of Israel, which has "gone mad" in its attempt to realize messianic and nationalistic dreams of redemption through violence.[45] In this context, Hana's bourgeois aspirations, for example, may be seen as expressing the general shift in Israel's economic and ideological orientation from the early socialist ideal to industrial capitalism.[46] Such a reading of My Michael would suggest that the real threat to Israel's existence and sovereignty lies not across the border, in the "lands of the Jackal," but rather inside the camp itself. In this scheme of things, from a connotational perspective, woman emblematizes the self-destructive impulse which Amos Oz perceives to be Israel's real problem.

CHAPTER 5

Gynographic Re-visions: Amalia Kahana-Carmon

The Woman Author as Other

While there seems to be a critical consensus about the technical and stylistic innovativeness of Amalia Kahana-Carmon, the most highly respected woman author in Israel, it is not difficult to detect some reservation about the importance of her work. It is no coincidence that the decision to grant her the 1985 Brenner Prize (third in rank after the Bialik and the Israel Prize for belles lettres) was mostly based on a recognition of her "sensitivity to the word, the rigor, the precision, the scrupulousness in the choice of the word: the word in its widest narrative meaning," rather than on an appreciation for the "word's" meaning or significance.[1] The laudatory emphasis on *how* she writes evokes ever so subtly the critical reticence about *what* she writes. Even in this most unlikely context, Kahana-Carmon is declared to have the ability to create pretty rather than important fiction.[2]

The critical ambivalence towards Kahana-Carmon's work can be traced back to the generally sympathetic response to her first collection of short stories, *Under One Roof* (1966). While the stories were praised as technical triumphs, several reviews pointed out that for the most part they were "merely love stories."[3] Instead of pointing to Kahana-Carmon's innovative treatment of heterosexual love stories and the genre of romance, sympathetic critics tended to minimize the role of those themes, preferring to dwell on the "universal" aspect of the "human" encounter (that is, what has traditionally been ratified as relevant to "man"), or on its metaphysical and religious aspects (as in the interpretation of her stories as exemplifications of Buber's concept of the I-Thou relationship).[4] Kahana-Carmon's first novel, *And Moon in the Valley of*

87

Ajalon (1971), was also generally praised for its artistic achievements, often by the same critics who pointed out its thematic limited scope.[5] The novel's defenders argued that it was not "really" concerned with a married woman's predicaments, but with the archetypal battle between the "saint and the dragon."[6] In a similar vein, those who defended her triptych, *Magnetic Fields* (1977), against the criticisms of its excessive sophistication and thematic anemia interpreted the work as a fictionalization of such mystical moments as the desire to transcend reality through death.[7] But despite the apparently sharp disagreements between Kahana-Carmon's critics and her eulogizers, both sides essentially agree that Kahana-Carmon's ideas and thematic materials are unimportant. While her critics reject as trivial her female characters and their problems, her defenders allegorize them.

This is not to say that Kahana-Carmon's work is not concerned with the anatomy of human encounters, the desire to be at the top, the search for transcendence, or the relationship between life and art. My argument is that these motifs can and ought to be seen as thematic extensions of the female predicament Kahana-Carmon describes. The allegorization of that predicament posits a substitutional and hierarchical relationship between the female and the human condition which implies that the latter is not only different from the former, but more important. It is not clear to me why, as overtly an androcentric novel as Pinhas Sadeh's *Life as a Parable* (1958), not only presents itself as addressing universal and human problems, but is readily accepted as doing so, while Kahana-Carmon's stories are immediately perceived as at best marginal. A plausible reason for this critical reaction is suggested by Amalia Kahana-Carmon herself: "With us, especially with us, it is so established that the main road of traditional Hebrew literature moves along the pivots that are built on the social and psychological values and the goals of Mr. Pencil throughout his generations, in accordance with the manner in which Mr. Pencil finds himself as a person, in the world at a given time."[8] Because Mr. Pencil, or the Hebrew male author, is likely to be perceived as the "*Shliah Tsibur*," who represents the community during services, his fiction is likely to be evaluated as a major document that expresses larger social concerns. Mrs. Pencil will at best be seen as Mr. Pencil's helpmate, and her fiction is likely to be categorized as women's literature: "a department which functions as a partner for that which is the ideational backbone of Hebrew literature. A partner—yes, the thing itself—not exactly."[9]

The tendency of Amalia Kahana-Carmon's defenders to apologize for the high visibility of female characters and her critics' charges concerning her allegedly limited scope are based on a literary tradition which identifies universality with masculinity. The cornerstone of phallic criticism, this tradition informs not only Hebrew literary tradition, but, as has been demonstrated, the Western literary establishment in general.[10] The alleged triviality of Kahana-Carmon's subject matter is the product of a male-centered value system which devalues women's writing, women as fictional characters, and women's real or imagined concerns. My argument is that there is no need to dignify Kahana-Carmon's work by resorting to convoluted allegorical interpretations. There is no need to justify her inclusion in the canon by "universalizing" her stories.[11] The critical "rehabilitation" of Kahana-Carmon by her defenders discloses their agreement with their apparent opponents that female characters are not as universal as male characters and that women's traditional concerns are not as significant as men's concerns. Virginia Woolf described the fallacious thinking of androcentric critics thus: "This is an important book, the critic assumes, because it deals with war. This is an insignificant book because it deals with the feelings of women in a drawing-room. A scene in a battlefield is more important than a scene in a shop—everywhere and much more subtly the difference of value persists."[12]

The dismissive attitude toward the contents of Kahana-Carmon's fiction may explain the few serious attempts made to explore the relationship between her thematics and her poetics. Her tendency to place perception before action, consciousness before plot, and suggestive narration before clarity indicates more than a mere susceptibility to Uri Nissan Gnessin and S. Yizhar's interior monologues.[13] A more careful consideration of Kahana-Carmon's thematic world will reveal how much she shares with Dvorah Baron (1887–1970), the first Hebrew woman author who often focused on the victimization of women in the patriarchal Jewish European shtetl, and Nehama Puhachevsky (1869–1934), the foremost woman writer of the first Aliya (immigration wave), who described, among other things, the struggles of female pioneers in Palestine.[14] Placing Amalia Kahana-Carmon's work in the context of her women predecessors and contemporaries like Yehudith Hendel, Naomi Fraenkel, Miriam Schwartz, Rachel Eytan, Ruth Almog, Dahlia Rabikovitch, and Yael Medini may help disabuse critics of the current tendency to consider her as an exception, an Other. As Carmon herself puts it: "To be the outsider: the one who is not a member of the club. This Brenner's wife [the woman writer] is the one whose work is predestined to remain outside any labeled drawer. She sees herself as one who was miraculously chosen, or doomed, depending on the point of view, to be totally outside the system."[15]

This is not to suggest that Kahana-Carmon must be considered only in the context of women writers or that women writers share a certain feminine sensibility that distinguishes them from male writers.[16] To a

certain extent, scholars like Nurith Gertz, who situate Kahana-Carmon's
work outside the mainstream of both the Palmah Generation and the
Generation of Statehood, are right, for Kahana-Carmon's thematics and
poetics do indeed defy easy categorization.[17] On the other hand, by
presenting her work as exceptional, we risk defining it as Other, as an
easy target for isolation and even elimination. For, as Joanna Russ points
out, false categorization—or noncategorization, for that matter—have
traditionally been frequent rationalizations for excluding women's
works from the canon.[18] The rationale for marginalizing Yehudith
Hendel's gynography as a Palmah author is the same one that risks
marginalizing Kahana-Carmon's as an author of the Generation of
Statehood: both gynographies do not "fit" the thematic and poetic agendas of their respective generations. By considering Kahana-Carmon's
work in the context of other female writers, we stand to gain a better
understanding of her concerns, her thematics. A better understanding
of her thematics will also shed light on her poetics.

For, like Dvorah Baron, Kahana-Carmon is vitally interested in the
female condition. Her experimental writing is directly related to her interest in female charcters and in the female condition on the one hand,
and to her awareness of the dismissive attitude towards them on the
other. By focusing on the consciousness of her introspective characters
and by de-emphasizing, even obscuring, action and plot sequences,
Kahana-Carmon has created the literary instruments necessary for an
unprecedented literary examination of the allegedly uninspiring lives of
"traditional" women.

Kahana-Carmon's redefinition of action as "the moment before the
action" or "the longing for, or recoiling from, or the gentleness
surrounding one's relationships" is vitally related to her interest in the
female outsider who has been banished from the sphere of action.[19] By
avoiding the linear, causal plot progression with its focus on a beginning,
a climax, and a denouement and by focusing instead on the drama of
consciousness, she is not only challenging the poetic principles of
realistic drama, but is redefining the meaning of narrative action. By including desires, intentions, and plans ("the moment before the action") as
well as fears, misgivings, or doubts ("recoiling from action") in the
category of action, Kahana-Carmon is expanding its meaning to include
the perceptual and emotional events that shape even as they disturb the
lives of her otherwise passive characters. Instead of the dramatic
paradigm, Kahana-Carmon prefers a loosely connected plot line con-
sisting of intense epiphanic episodes. As she puts it, her stories revolve
around "a picture urgently addressing the sacredness of the day-to-day.
This picture [is becoming] a harbor for a wonderous cruise toward a mo-

ment of revelation" (*Roof*, p. 241). The "strobe light" technique il-
luminating single moments in a continuum of a character's daily routine
enables us to perceive the uniqueness and even "sacredness" in what one
would tend to shirk off as the trivial activities of, for example, a traditional homemaker.[20]

Kahana-Carmon's interest in traditional female role models as
literary subjects may also illuminate her unique technique of
characterization. Although she rejects the heroic model of the Palmah
Generation, she does not espouse the ironic or symbolic approach of the
New Wave writers. While her protagonists are social outcasts who share
something in common with the impotent and alienated outsiders of
Amos Oz and A.B. Yehoshua, they are neither satirized nor used as national or social symbols. Despite their weakness, they emerge as
heroines and heroes in the original sense of the word. Mr. Hiram, the
author's poetic alter ego in *And Moon in the Valley of Ajalon*, answers an
imaginary question about the weakness of his characters thus: "It
depends on how you interpret them. I do not think that they [my
characters] are weak people. They are exposed. They lack a certain cor-
tex. To permit themselves not to develop it testifies ultimately to another
[kind of] strength. A strength they essentially had. But one which
became eroded, due to the circumstances."[21] Nurith Gertz sees Kahana-
Carmon's empathetic characterization of her alienated protagonists as a
manifestation of her simultaneous participation in the Palmah Generation, her "biological" contemporaries, and the Generation of Statehood,
her "poetic" contemporaries.[22] However, we must also consider Kahana-
Carmon's uncommon interest in female characters. The new poetic
grammar she creates is closely related to her implicit challenge to the
dismissive and punitive approaches to female characters in both the
Palmah Generation and the New Wave.

Kahana-Carmon's revisionary project is also closely related to her
widely respected "high" style.[23] Her unique use of metaphor and simile,
her euphuisms, biblicisms and archaisms, and her unconventional use of
grammar and syntax (all of which makes it so difficult to translate her
work) are well suited to her attempt to elevate, dignify, and even mystify
what has traditionally been considered unimportant. Kahana-Carmon's
use of a solemn, nuanced, and allusive style to present, for example, a
budding female poet in her teens challenges the tendency of male Israeli
writers to present girls as brainless or unselfconscious sex objects. For
although we realize that her heroines are mostly focalizers who may not
speak or think in the implied author's terms, we *are* expected to believe
that the sensibility and subtlety implied by the language are there.
Kahana-Carmon's use of "high" Hebrew is closely related to her revi-

sionary treatment of the private sphere, which has been marginalized and devalued in both the Palmah Generation and the Generation of Statehood.[24]

But Kahana-Carmon's revisionary perspective has ineluctable limits, largely because of the tenacity of androcentric doctrines, the price of revisionary writing (especilly in a heavily androcentric context), and the dialectical relationship between the denigration and valorization of similar female images. For, as we shall see, her sympathetic treatment of traditional women may sometimes be read as an implicit idealization of their vulnerability and dependence on men. As I shall argue later, inspiring as it may be, the focus on the heroine's social inferiority may be seen as an implicit affirmation of woman's traditional enclosure within a male-dominated economy. Kahana-Carmon's insistence on the heroine's consciousness at the expense of her body implicitly validates the Victorian identification of female virtue with propriety, that is, asexuality.[25] Even if we accept that Kahana-Carmon's evasion of the body is a response to the dominant literary tendency to ignore female spirituality, we should not remain blind to the price of this inspired and important response, and to the ways in which it may share the common premises of androcentrism. As in Naomi Fraenkel and Yehudith Hendel, for example, Kahana-Carmon's "good" heroine challenges the image of the male-authored treacherous helpmate. At the same time, the central role men play in the heroine's life may reinforce the androcentric perception about men's centrality in women's lives. Similarly, Kahana-Carmon's tendency to present her heroine's romantic involvements as quasi-religious experiences implicitly endorses the vision of heterosexual love as redemptive. The presentation of male lovers as potential redeemers underwrites the mystification of phallic power, as expressed, for example, in D.H. Lawrence's work.[26]

Nevertheless, Kahana-Carmon's work stands out as the most consistent challenge to the androcentric gyniconology of the Other. By restoring conscience and consciousness to the mimetic aspect of the female image and by studying its complexities, she is challenging the androcentric tendency to present woman as a void, a sexual object or a male adjunct. Like Yehudith Hendel before her, Amalia Kahana-Carmon's gynographies create a plausible illusion of femaleness as Selfhood. By attending to the restrictions imposed on women, she debunks the gyniconological representations of women as inherently malicious.

In *And Moon in the Valley of Ajalon* (1971) and in her latest novel, *Up in Montifer* (1984), Kahana-Carmon dwells on the victimization of women by patriarchal arrangements. Of course, she is not the first or only woman author to have done so. As already noted, women figure as victims in female-authored works from Dvorah Baron to Miriam Schwartz (*The Story of Eve Gotlieb*, 1968), Shulamith Har-Even (*Loneliness*, 1980), Ruth Almog (*The Stranger and the Enemy*, 1980), and Shulamit Gingold-Gilboa (*Either Winter or Its End*, 1981). Thus far, however, I think it is right to consider Kahana-Carmon's gynography as the most sensitive and original attempt to record the victimization(s) of women in a patriarchal economy.

As we shall see, her work moves from the romantic antiromantic stories of *Under One Roof* (1966), through a sensitive depiction of the double bind of a married woman in *And Moon in the Valley of Ajalon* (1971), to a tentative and partial exploration of the image of the independent woman in *Magnetic Fields* (1977). One could argue that by portraying most of her heroines as dependent on males and as victimized by them (Wendy in *Magnetic Fields* is a secondary character), Kahana-Carmon risks idealizing the image and state of the female victim. When the female's rehabilitation requires a sympathetic vision, the combination of female heroism and victimization becomes problematic. A careful reading of Kahana-Carmon's work can demonstrate, however, that the valorization of the female Other often results in a critique of the repressive conditions that lead to her victimization. The more sympathetic the heroine's treatment, the more objectionable her oppression.

For Amalia Kahana-Carmon is not only struggling with the female Other as a literary image, but also with her self-image as Other in a male-dominated canon. As the first (and thus far only) woman author to gain partial access to the Hebrew literary canon, she is facing a tough struggle against a literary establishment that often identifies creativity with masculinity. Even women poets like Rachel, Leah Goldberg, Yocheved Bat Miriam, Zelda, Dahlia Rabikovitch, and Yona Wallach, who apparently fared better than women prose writers, are considered second-class citizens. As the poet David Avidan put it in a recent article protesting what he condemned as the excessive eulogies shortly after Yona Wallach's untimely death: "Wallach competed on the race track of the *women poets* [italics in original] . . . Wallach tried to compete—with less success—on the race track of the *male poets* [italics in original], and there she is not in my opinion a serious competitor."[27]

As one of a handful of prose writers who have ventured to write in a language reserved for men until the turn of the century, Kahana-Carmon and her female contemporaries (not to speak of her predecessors) are facing the same struggle for legitimacy that their nineteenth century English counterparts faced.[28] As Margaret Homans explains: "To be for so long the other and the object made it difficult for nineteenth century women to have their own subjectivity. To become a

poet, given these conditions, required nothing less than battling a valued
and loved literary tradition, to forge a self out of the materials of
otherness. It is not surprising that so few women succeeded at this effort; very few even conceived of the possibility of trying."[29] The contemporary Hebrew writer must struggle not only with defeating traditional
female images, but with discouraging cultural perceptions about
woman's proper place. The struggle is both external and internal. The
Hebrew woman author must not only face a male-dominated literary
establishment and tradition that tend to dismiss women's writings as
Other, but she must also struggle with the androcentric perceptions and
value judgments she herself has imbibed from her culture and society.
For even the contemporary Israeli women authors who are aware of
their status as Other, or, as Kahana-Carmon puts it, of the automatic
dismissal of their work as "wasted on the peripheral, on the ultimately
unimportant, and on the trivial," are not exempt from the "value
judgments that are [so] destructive to them."[30] The self-awareness of
Israeli authors as Others is itself a hindrance, for "a priori they recognize
without a doubt that even at their best, there will be an identity, and a
perception, and an order [of priorities], and a voice, that are less
weighty, and go less far, and answer a need that is less deep than those
men writers may achieve when they are at their best."[30]

It should come as no surprise that Kahana-Carmon's gynography,
despite her ability to articulate so well the contradictions and problems
entailed in female writing, manifests the residual impacts of androcentric thinking.[31] In the following pages, we shall see how Kahana-Carmon
struggles with these conventions, especially in the context of her early
fiction.

Under One Roof: The Antiromantic Romantic Story

As noted in the introduction, those of Kahana-Carmon's defenders
who have attempted to either minimize or deny her insistence on the
theme of heterosexual relationships seem to have missed two points.
Firstly, the theme of heterosexual love is central in both the Palmah
Generation and the Generation of Statehood. The main difference between the male-authored narratives and those of Amalia Kahana-Carmon
in this regard seems to lie in Kahana-Carmon's focus on, and sympathetic
treatment of, the female partner. In addition, unlike the numerous male-
authored *belles dames sans merci*, Kahana-Carmon's perceptive heroines
experience love as an epiphanic moment. This is not to say that *Under
One Roof* subscribes to the traditional romantic vision of heterosexual

love or marriage. Although she does not quite go "beyond the ending" to offer an alternative denouement to her heroines' lives, Kahana-Carmon defies the romantic happy ending of the traditional romance.[32] As we shall see, she shuns both the euphoric and the catastrophic vision of romantic love. The structural atomization of the romantic encounter redefines not only the conventional romantic plot, but also common perceptions of heterosexual love, to the point of declaring that this love is impossible, if not completely illusory. At the same time, she avoids what the poet Nathan Zach calls "the romantic double bind" which plagues so much of modern Hebrew literature, with its visible suscep-tibility to acts of violence, betrayal, divorce, and such catastrophic en-dings as suicide, fatal diseases and accidents, murder, death in battle, or death in childbirth. Kahana-Carmon's kind of story may perhaps be best understood as the romantic antiromantic story.[33]

In his effort to prove that Kahana-Carmon is really referring to much more important matters than romantic love, Avraham Balaban, expand-ing Gershon Shaked's interpretation, argues that *Under One Roof* ex-emplifies Martin Buber's concept of the I-Thou relationship.[34] But even the most cursory glance at Buber's treatment of the I-Thou relationship reveals its inadequacy as a hermeneutical key for Kahana-Carmon's treatment of predominantly heterosexual encounters. While Buber in-sists on the I-Thou relationship as an objective, reciprocal event, Kahana-Carmon is mostly interested in the encounter as a subjective or even completely imaginary event which is rarely if ever reciprocal.[35] For ex-ample, Dr. Orbank in "Impoverishment" is barely aware of the nameless heroine's internal turmoil during their meeting in a restaurant, just as it is never clear whether the amorous encounter between Dr. Bruchin and Mrs. Sokolow in "The Heart of the Summer, the Heart of the Light" has ever taken place or whether it is an imaginative projection of the child narrator, Ronen. Similarly, while Buber insists on the nonparticular character of "Thou" as a potential representative of the human race, Kahana-Carmon's usually male "Thou" is described as a unique, often ex-ceptional, individual. For Mrs. Amsterdam, the commercial cor-respondence teacher in "If You Please," the Orthodox clerk becomes for a single night a mysterious "man living on a star" (*Roof*, pp. 101, 103, 108, 115). For Carmela in "Painted Pictures," Yohanan is described as the "one and only" (*Roof*, p. 72). The heroine of "Neima Sasson Writes Poems" thinks that her teacher, Yehezkel da Silva, is "separate, different, unique" (*Roof*, p. 143), just as Hava for Yehoshua in "On the Street" is "different from all the rest" (*Roof*, p. 76). While Buber warns that as long as love is "blind"—that is, as long as it does not see a *whole* being—it does not yet truly stand under the basic word of relation" (*I and Thou*, p. 68),

Kahana-Carmon's heroines emphatically do not "see" their partners in the Buberian sense. Noa in "I am Thirsty for your Waters Jerusalem" does not know Asher any more than Pua knows Iov in "A White Goat, a Bindtree, a Path of Casuarines." Avigail's attraction to Steven in "Winning from Free" and Bruno's unadmitted fascination with Erika in "Under One Roof" and "A Trip Before Evening" are just as "blind" as the intense, but evanescent kinship between Ilana and Noa in "Be'er Sheba the Negev's Capital" or between Tirtsa and Enokh in "From the Sights of the Stairs Painted Bright Blue." Finally, as we shall see, Kahana-Carmon's encounters, no matter how intense, are also inevitably transient. And although they exist as inspiring memories in the protagonist's mind, they do not turn into the permanent presence Buber is describing.

It is indeed ironic that Buber's I-Thou relationship, which is so clearly defined in contrast to the romantic paradigm, should be taken as the hermeneutic key to Kahana-Carmon's stories. For although romantic love is redefined, challenged, and revised in important ways in these stories, it nevertheless functions as a central paradigm. To resort to such respectable but incongruous concepts as Buber's I-Thou relationship mystifies and obfuscates Kahana-Carmon's stories. The attempt to substitute the heterosexual with a religious paradigm is indicative of the axiological prioritization of the religious paradigm and of the critical tendency to allegorize literary mythogynies.

It is possible, on the other hand, that the impulse to interpret Kahana-Carmon's text in a religious or mystical light stems from the author's tendency to describe in mystical terms the intensity with which the romantic moment registers on the consciousness of her heroines. But then, as Denis de Rougemont has pointed out, the Western interpretation of romantic love shares both structural and historical affinities with religious (notably Christian) mysticism.[36] In other words, there is no need to create a substitutive or oppositional relationship between romance and mysticism in the context of Kahana-Carmon's gynographies. Such familiar moments as the uncontrollable power drawing the lovers to each other, their lack of real knowledge about each other, the mutual devotion to the exclusion of other concerns or people, the scant verbal and sexual communication between them, the failure to establish a stable and lasting communion, and the unavoidable misunderstandings and ensuing pain and separations are, as de Rougemont notes, secular manifestations of medieval doctrines about the soul's relationship to God.

I am insisting on the role of the romantic paradigm in Kahana-Carmon's work because much of the power and importance of her gynography lies in her revisionary approach to that paradigm. For although all of the above-mentioned moments appear in her romantic subplots, those subplots lack the element of reciprocity which makes up the traditional romantic mythos. It is not simply that her stories deal with the mythos of unrequited love, but that the participants in the romantic event seem to emote at cross-purposes, at the wrong time, at the wrong place, whenever their partner seems least interested, aware, or accessible. The romantic encounter is atomized into unstable moments of attraction, paralysis, and flight to an extent which renders questionable the implied solidity or stability of such ideas as 'relationship' or 'love.' Nevertheless, the author celebrates the romantic encounter as a revitalizing experience of "enchantment," and her heroines' fleeting encounters with their male counterparts are often framed as wishful projections (as in "The Heart of Summer, the Heart of the Light") or as reconstructive idealizations of the past (as in "Be'er Sheba the Negev's Capital").[37] In the final analysis, the romantic moment emerges in these stories as illusive. Its powerful impact derives from the heroine's awareness of her feelings rather than from the knight's performance. The celebration of what emerges as not only painful but also as transient and illusory may best be described as Amalia Kahana-Carmon's "antiromantic romantic story."

While pseudoeuphoric stories like "Neima Sasson Writes Poems," "If I Found Favor in Your Eyes," "Painted Postcards," "From the Sights of the Stairs Painted Bright Blue," and "Impoverishment" present the princess of romance as a woman who desperately tries and fails to make contact with an unresponsive or unreliable knight, pseudodysphoric stories like "To Build Herself a Home in the Land of Shinar," "Under One Roof," and "A Trip Before Evening" avoid the tragic denouement of conventional stories about stultifying marriages.[38] The pseudoeuphoric romance lacks the happy ending, and the heroine usually loses her beloved. The pseudodysphoric story foregoes the catastrophic ending (death, suicide, elopement) that is especially typical of the male-authored Israeli story. In such stories as "A White Goat, a Bindtree, a Path of Casuarines" and "The Heart of the Summer, the Heart of the Light," both plot patterns merge.

"Neima Sasson Writes Poems" is a good example of the pseudoeuphoric romance. The eponymous heroine is an adolescent student at an Orthodox school for girls. The knight is her married teacher Yehezkel da Silva. Neima is desperately trying to draw Yehezkel's attention: "I in the new summer dress for which I had so many hopes. The teacher Yehezkel is already sitting without motion . . . and I knew once again that everything is lost" (*Roof*, p. 136). but Neima is not deterred by her failures. Again and again she tries to make contact with her beloved teacher. She takes "everyday the wrong bus" so as to be able to sit or stand by him (pp. 137–138). She walks by his house, watches his wife, and spends all her evenings at the back balcony of her parents' house waiting for him to show up. But: "The teacher Yehezkel does not come. He never comes" (p. 140). When she tries to confront him, to confess to him her secret ("One more question. Only one. Teacher Yehezkel, tell me, are you really unique?" p. 143), he dodges: "I do not think that I am a unique person. But everyone is for himself unique. So I am unfit to testify" (p. 144). Despairing of verbal communication, Neima turns to writing: "I do not know how to express in words. I therefore tried to convey in writing" (p. 144). But the poem "My Dear Teacher," which is accepted for publication by the school paper, is coldly shrugged off by Yehezkel da Silva, as are the other poems Neima entrusts to him: "The poems. I opened to read. I read about two pages. And I fell asleep" (p. 146). Like other pseudoeuphoric stories, "Neima Sasson Writes Poems" affirms that the knight in shining armor never responds to the calls of the enchanted princess—in other words, that romantic love cannot be realized. The only proper place for it is the heroine's consciousness, or her poetry.

And yet it is never too certain that Yehezkel da Silva is disinterested in Neima Sasson. Shortly after the teacher indicates he will not break the rules ("One Neima Sasson, one Yehezkel da Silva will fit themselves to the rules please," p. 149), he turns around, and Neima thinks: "He returned to me" (p. 149). The zigzagging dance that ensues epitomizes the fluctuating emotional movements alternately distancing and bringing together the participants:" He went off. I hurried on. "He went off. Stopped. Went on. I did not move. I hurried on. He stopped. He went off. I stood. He is going off, turning around. He came back" (p. 150). The lack of directional markers increases the indeterminacy of the fragile and ever-shifting "relationship." What emerges from this confusing dance is the possibility that the knight has been holding back out of fear rather than disinterest. Neima's willingness to be rejected and hurt again and again, humiliating herself "for the millionth time" (p. 140), is in fact a kind of courage that may point us in the direction of "the secret that turns the weak one into a hero" (pp. 144, 149).

The constantly shifting distance in "If I Found Favor in Your Eyes" between an Orthodox clerk in his twenties and Mrs. Amsterdam, a middle-class, married, commercial correspondence teacher, follows the same nervous rhythm of Neima and Yehezkel's dance. Here too, the first encounter between teacher and student is suffused with hope. Mrs. Amsterdam, the protagonist-narrator, thinks: "He is flying towards me. With stretched out, taut wings, and unseeing eyes" (*Roof*, p. 102). In "reality," the nameless man only offers her the right change as she is about to make a telephone call shortly before the beginning of the class.

This indeterminacy, the constantly shifting relationships between subjective and objective truth, control the story's rhythm. On the one hand, Mrs. Amsterdam emerges as a misguided romantic woman in search of what she calls "the man living on a star" (pp. 101, 103). On the other hand, her encounter with the man confirms her vision of him—on the single rainy evening they spend together—as nothing less than "the center" of her life (p. 106).

The zigzagging dance begins slowly, becoming increasingly hectic as the plot unfolds. In an attempt to make contact with the mysterious man living on a star, Mrs. Amsterdam follows him after class and begins to go through the motions of polite conversation (p. 104). Since her husband is out of town, she asks the man to see a film with her (pp. 105–107), confessing finally her true feelings for him: " 'I told you, you are a mysterious man,' I said sadly" (p. 108). Like Yehezkel, the mysterious man retreats soon after the magic moment. They buy their tickets; the Yeshiva student wishes to go home: "I always go this way. Good Night" (p. 108). But like Yehezkel da Silva, he returns. When she reaches her home, Mrs. Amsterdam discovers him standing on her steps, and runs toward him: "How didn't I notice. Wet. Because of me. For me. Without his books" (p. 111). "The man living on a star" returns, but does not explain why, saying, "I too do not know why [I came]" (p. 112). Mrs. Amsterdam joins her student on a bus ride back to his home, at which point he confesses in a roundabout way his special feelings for her, or rather for the special bond between them: "You said it yourself, I felt I was like Cain, after the deed with Abel. Abel—is not you. [It is] you and I" (p. 114). This admission, however, paves the way to their final separation, for shortly afterwards the mysterious man gets off the bus to return home ("They do not teach chivalry at the yeshiva," p. 114), letting Mrs. Amsterdam find her way home alone.

Mrs. Amsterdam is disappointed, but not crushed. Like Neima Sasson, she is strangely invigorated despite her momentary disillusionment. Seemingly reconciled to her separation from the mysterious young man, she offers an "objective" response to an imaginary interviewer asking her about her mysterious partner: "Ah, this one. Well, yes. Why not, [I have] a good opinion [of him]" (p. 115). But the narrative does not end on this dispassionate note. The story's concluding sentence validates the mystery of the evanescent encounter and reaffirms the image of the beloved man as an unforgettable memory: "And I, forever, forever will remember how he sat, not here, and with a chin resting on his chest as if reciting something" (p. 115).

If the romantic encounter fails as reality, it emerges victorious as a memory. It therefore does not matter that Mrs. Amsterdam loses "the

man living on a star," or that Neima Sasson never makes real contact
with Yehezkel da Silva. It does not matter that the intimate moment between Avigail and Ted in "Winning from Free," or between Tirtsa and
Enokh in "From the Sights of the House with the Stairs Painted Bright
Blue" is evanescent. What matters is that for these heroines, as for Ilana
in "Be'er Sheba the Negev's Capital" and for Carmela in "Painted
Postcards," the memory of the experienced contact overrides the fact of
the final separation. But the heroine's continued longing for the contact
turns her equanimity into the typically ambiguous closure of the
pseudoeuphoric plot.

Kahana-Carmon's gynography implodes the normative rules
underlying the dysphoric plot as well. Her focus on her heroine's subjective consciousness at the expense of details about what we might define
as "objective reality" may explain not only why the rejected princess continues to hold on to her dream, but also why the dejected queen prefers
to stay in her suffocating dungeon. Like Erika in "Under One Roof,"
Pua in "A White Goat, a Bindtree, a Path of Casuarines," and Hulda in
"The Heart of the Summer, the Heart of the Light," the nameless heroine
of "To Build Herself a Home in the Land of Shinar" is a middle-class
housewife alienated from her husband: "Her marriage did not turn out
well. But life continued in its tracks. Her husband used to come at night,
a stranger, not participating in the domestic life, sinking into the sofa by
the radio, turning the receiver's knobs and finally falling asleep there in
his clothes and shoes, until he would wake up and go to bed. His world
he did not share with her" (*Roof*, p. 95). Like Mrs. Peretz in "The Bright
Light," who finds herself isolated in an English countryside, our
nameless heroine, a Sephardic immigrant, is disconnected from the new
Israeli development town where she hoped to find a new home: "Real
neighbors she did not have either. Only the old Mr. Azulai and his
daughter Yocheved" (p. 95). Like Bruria, who makes peace with her constricting marriage and empty domestic life, our heroine too seems
resigned to her fate. She rejects the pragmatic approach ("It is a question
of labor organization," p. 99) offered by her guest, the big, blue-eyed
"beautiful and independent" (p. 96) specialist for nutrition and home
economics. She says: "No. This is life. Fate" (p. 99). When the specialist
suggests that she might find work outside the home, our heroine
counters, "After sixteen years of marriage I need courage" (p. 99). She
seems to imply, however, that pragmatic solutions are incompatible with
life's real problems. After all, a much greater move, immigrating to a
new country, did not stop the inevitable deterioration of her marriage:
" 'A new country, a new life, ha?' she said with empty hands" (p. 99).

Yet a careful reading of "To Build Herself a Home in the Land of Shinar" reveals that the heroine's disillusionment hides a certain hopefulness. The understanding that everything is relative and unstable mitigates the heroine's dejection, just as it dampens the enthusiasm of her counterparts in the pseudoeuphoric story. In addition, as is typical of Kahana-Carmon's gynographies, the focus on the heroine's subjective life destabilizes the meaning of what we might consider her failure in building herself a house (beginning a new life?) in Israel. The heroine experiences a recurring childhood memory with a far greater intensity than she does her social contacts. This memory celebrates a moment in her childhood when she visited a luminously bright hospital ward. Her recreation of the past ("And all the three nurses united into one figure, burning in a white fire," p. 96) vies for dominion with her present sense of defeat, apparently augmented by the visit of the beautiful professional woman. She lets herself experience, despite her disillusionment with her marital life, the subtle overtures of her long-estranged husband: "As a swift arrow the words [of her husband] went through her. After all, he did not address her in a very long time . . . 'It was not easy for him to speak to me but he is making an effort nonetheless'—a kind of fear, hesitation she heard in his voice. She waited to see what would happen. She was wondering if the specialist was noticing. And her heart was beating inside her like a hammer" (p. 98).[39] Shortly after the protagonist confesses to the specialist ("Nobody knew how stunning this confession was") that she had lost interest in cooking, she remembers an epiphanic moment of great beauty when her children showed her a white boat gliding on the clear blue sea (p. 98).

In view of the heroine's modest triumphs, or rather what she interprets as such, it is difficult to categorize her mythogyny as dysphoric. The story seems to challenge the mythogyny of the victimized, passive woman by celebrating her subjectivities. The heroine's resignation discloses a different kind of heroism, one not commonly found in male-authored mythogynies. The secret, turning a weakling into a hero, is the ability to embrace with gratitude the little joys of life and to open oneself up to the hidden significance, even mystery, couched in what appear to be pedestrian, routine events.

The ability to appreciate what others consider insignificant events explains the disinclination of Kahana-Carmon's heroine to rebel against her oppression. It is, among other things, this ability that renders superfluous the catastrophic ending of the conventional dysphoric story. Noticing her husband's efforts to serve dinner, our nameless heroine is overcome with unspeakable joy. Having been complimented

by the home economics specialist and her husband for the cleanliness of
the house," the heart of the mistress of the house was consumed inside
her, as after great deeds" (p. 100). By the end of the story, we realize that
the real "great deeds" invoked by the director of the town council at the
beginning of the story apply to the invisible struggles of the
unglamorous homemaker rather than to the efforts of the pioneering
settlers to build a new town. Thus Kahana-Carmon's gynographic
strategies permit the image of the housewife—trivialized and denigrated
in most androcentric Israeli fiction—to control the source of the story's
vitality.

Amalia Kahana-Carmon's gynography demonstrates both her attachment to, and defiance of, the Generation of Statehood. While it
challenges the traditional female-centered plot, it continues to present
the encounter with the male partner as a salvific moment, the starting
point of self-awareness. The feminization of the private sphere and the
mystification of the heterosexual encounter are pivotal to her fiction,
although they are thoroughly revised. By presenting the romantic encounter as superior to her heroine's other preoccupations, Kahana-
Carmon reinforces the traditional separation in Israeli fiction between
femaleness and the public sphere of action. Although she revises the
gyniconologies of her male counterparts, she subscribes in her early fiction to the ideology of romantic love and endorses its central role in her
mythogynies. For as Mary Poovey points out in her analysis of Jane
Austen, the presentation of romantic love as the center and climax of the
heroine's life reinforces the mythic model of private gratification as sufficient for women.[40]

But by focusing on the heroine's consciousness, Kahana-Carmon
challenges the androcentric perspective underlying her male counterparts' gyniconologies. Her attentiveness to the heroine's fluctuating
perceptions, hopes, fears, reflections, moral principles, and
psychological struggles endows the Hebrew heroine with what she has
been sorely deprived of in male-authored fiction: conscience and consciousness, a mind of her own. The innovativeness of a character like
Neima Sasson can only be appreciated when compared to the two-
dimensional beauties of S. Yizhar, the voluptuous adolescents of the early Moshe Shamir and Amos Oz, and the unattainable nymphets of A.B.
Yehoshua.[41] By combining the ability to love a man (and/or be loved by
him) and creative susceptibility in a female character, Kahana-Carmon is
defying the traditional opposition between the two capabilities (as in Oz's
repugnant poetess; Tova in "All the Rivers"; Sarah, the psychotic poetry
lover in Sadeh's Life as a parable; or Yehoshua's neurotic amateur, Dina,
in Late Divorce). The revisionary characterization of a married woman

like Mrs. Amsterdam can only be appreciated when juxtaposed with the vindictive treatment of adulterous or lecherous wives (such as Yitzhak Orpaz's Rachel in *Ants*, or Megged's Elisheva Green in *The Short Life*), and the caricaturing of professional women (such as Genia in Amos Oz's *My Michael* or Asya in A.B. Yehoshua's *The Lover*).

Nevertheless, the heroine's escape from a hostile social world to the poetry of daily routine, from the world into her own consciousness, is ultimately an escape into "a prisonhouse of sensibility."[42] Paradoxically, this escape conforms to the androcentric privatization of feminine space. To the extent that Kahana-Carmon's heroines sacrifice the "outside" to maintain their integrity, they valorize their imprisonment in romantic versions of the feminine. To the extent that this inner beauty constitutes the core of her heroism, the heroine can be seen as an extension of the perfect beauty of romance. The following quote from Rachel Brownstein's study of the twentieth century self-conscious heroine in the English and American novel is particularly appropriate here:

> The beautiful personal integrity the novel heroine imagines and stands for and seeks for herself is a version of the romantic view of woman as a desired object; as the image of the integral self, she is the inverted image of half of a couple. The literary associations that surround the heroine keep her in a traditional woman's place. That self-awareness which distinguishes her from the simple heroine of romance ends by implicating her further in fictions of the feminine. On the other hand, in the end I have only self awareness—the conscious heroine's pride and prison—to recommend as a solution to all these problems.[43]

In *And Moon in the Valley of Ajalon*, Kahana-Carmon shows a greater awareness of the price the heroine pays for her escape into her Self, the price of a rich and admirable but ultimately besieged Self.

CHAPTER 6

Self-Conscious Heroism: *And Moon in the Valley of Ajalon*

The Desire to Be at the Top

At one point in *And Moon in the Valley of Ajalon*, Mrs. Noa Talmor, the protagonist-narrator, compares the story of her life to "a story in installments from a ladies' journal. [The characters are] an Israeli industrialist, his wife, and a specialist from abroad. The industrialist shall we say [is] an industrialist. His wife [is] a broken person, lacking will power and self-respect. The specialist from abroad, but I would not know how to describe him to you, your honor the judge. He is a good person. A good person."[1] Addressed to an imaginary judge and jury, this ironic summary of events echoes the combination of the pseudoeuphoric and pseudodysphoric stories of *Under One Roof*. The euphoric encounter, or intimate relationship with the long-awaited prince ends with disillusionment, and the dysphoric marital story does not end violently. In the case of *And Moon in the Valley of Ajalon*, the heroine Mrs. Talmor, the wife of Asher Talmor, a successful businessman, meets Philip, a British engineer with whom she falls in love. This relationship does not last and the heroine remains locked up in her marriage—and in her consciousness.

The novel seems to fluctuate between a romantic vision which validates Noa Talmor's desire to match reality with her aspirations and an antiromantic vision which questions her typical "desire to be at the top" (pp. 72, 96, 97, 120, 156). (Noa is the heroine's name in chapter 3, which describes her as a young single woman; Mrs. Talmor is her name throughout the novel.) I do not agree, however, with Nissim Calderon, who suggests that this desire is the sin of hubris committed by the inexperienced Noa and paid for by Mrs. Talmor twenty years later.[2] While it may be naive to believe that dreams are realizable, it is not particularly realistic to interpret Mrs. Talmor's dreams as sinful. In a similar vein, the novel presents Mrs. Talmor's encounter with Philip both as a mystical, salvific moment and as an illusory, foredoomed one. What reinforces the latter interpretation is the juxtaposition of this encounter with Noa's encounter with Asher Talmor.

That both encounters end badly implies, among other things, that the heroine's true salvation lies elsewhere. But it is not altogether clear whether it lies in Mrs. Talmor's retreat into her consciousness, though her internal monologues and dialogues are often more intense and meaningful than her verbal communications with Philip, or the young Asher.

Mrs. Talmor escapes into her consciousness having realized that she cannot escape either from her oppressive marriage or from the competitive and pragmatic society epitomized by her opportunistic husband. Like Puah in "A White Goat, a Bindtree, a Path of Casuarines," Noa Talmor resigns herself to her oppressive marriage after one failed attempt to leave her husband: "The man cried. The woman stayed. And she does not know why. And she does not know how to define what she lost because of it. It was not much. But it was all that she had" (p. 39).

In her consciousness, Mrs. Talmor is free to identify herself with the demoted Russian Princess Anastasia, free to absorb the poetry of trivial details, free to form alliances with beloved people and objects, and free to despise her husband's social and economic success: "The touch of success. In order to succeed in business you must be infected. Infected with a unique inhumanness. In the businessman as a young man the inhumanness is a minute spot. During the day one does not notice it . . . [This is] a mistake: this spot, this tip of a pin, [this is] the essence of the man. This essence spreads gradually. A stranger would not notice, would not know. Only the wife sees" (p. 39).

Nevertheless, Noa Talmor is aware of both the inescapability and the price of her retreat into herself. In response to Philip's puzzlement at her subservience ("One question: in the car, why would you agree to sit in the back seat? Why for instance don't you simply refuse to travel?" p. 124), Mrs. Talmor says, "[This is] a small detail" (p. 124). But in one of several internal monologues which she silently addresses to Philip, Mrs. Talmor pleads her case thus: "A woman, who at least like any human being, at least in some areas, usually knows what she is talking about, is a priori considered to be babbling. First forgivingly, then with annoyance. In time, she must lose a certain trust in her strength. No longer a woman who knows what she is talking about" (p. 108). Mrs. Talmor understands her retreat as a tactic of self-defense against her insensitive husband, as well as the sorry result of an eroded sense of self, a lack of confidence.

Despite her tendency to put personal integrity before social sanction, Mrs. Talmor is aware of the price she pays for her priorities. Though she tries to convince Philip that being publicly humiliated by her husband "does not hurt anymore" (p. 94), she is aware that she still "chokes when they rob you of the possibility of feeling that you are a good woman, a proud woman" (p. 108).[3]

But if Mrs. Talmor's internal monologues and imaginary dialogues explain her point of view to the reader, they are not available to Asher Talmor, who remains throughout the novel untouched by his wife's struggles, indeed unaware of the constant activity of her brilliant mind. Irritated by what he considers her antisocial conduct, and rejecting her tendency to asocial behavior as foolhardy, Asher often chastises his wife: "Did you know that you are a feeble-minded woman, fickle, never content and untidy? . . . [You are] a gloomy woman, an obstinate woman, uncompromising. Four feet in the ground and even from there [you] believe that for candidness and sincerity one deserves a prize . . . A ridiculous woman, an anachronism, I say" (p. 103). For the successful businessman, Mrs. Talmor's uncompromising devotion to "candidness and sincerity" is a mere display of obstinacy, "an anachronism." For a man like Asher, who assesses everything by its lucrative potential, Mrs. Talmor's refusal to participate in the social game is ridiculous and infantile. When Mrs. Talmor refuses to use her "social connections" with, for example, her nameless erstwhile colleague from the Palmah, he admonishes and later dismisses her (pp. 71–93).

Yet Mrs. Talmor is aware that Asher is not the main cause of her distress. At one point she admits to Asher and his partner Mr. Rothman that she did not appreciate properly what she had as a young married woman: "The girls were small and sweet. The days were young. The dresses were pretty. People, nice, as usual. Asher, and working so hard, providing comfortably. How is it that I to enjoy all these, that the light is sweet to the eyes, did not manage. With a boiling, burning, restless head, where was I?" (p. 67). Mrs. Talmor is admitting here that it was not the sordid reality of social hypocrisy that began the deterioration of her marriage, but rather her own restless yearning for more. Yet she is not quite capable of defining that yearning. Thinking back to an even earlier phase in her relationship with Asher, the moment she sees as "the peak of [her] life" (p. 30), she wonders: "What did I want? What did I ask for? What did I ask of the future?" (p. 31).

But a glance at the period Mrs. Talmor considers the peak of her life reveals that even as a young student in the enchanting city of Jerusalem she was anxious and worried that her experiences were not real: "At times, it seemed that this was not real life, but only its less complex paradigm, fit for [her] measurements; perhaps [only] an admission ticket to the future" (p. 43). The mature Mrs. Talmor realizes that there was folly in her youthful yearnings for more, in her desire to be at the top. Addressing an invisible, unknown judge (as she often does throughout the novel), she admits that her greatest folly was to expect that life would continue to unfold in a series of climactic moments: "Your honor the judge, the interesting thing is how, simultaneously came the turn of the enthusiastic assumption: from now on this peak [is] the usual plateau. From it [the peak] to fly up to other peaks, who knows, to the sky" (p. 72).

Despite her belated realization of the folly ingrained in her will to be at the top, she does not quite give it up, as we see most clearly in her relationship with Philip. Like Dr. Bruchin and "the man living on a star," Philip appears to the heroine as "the bright winter day" (p. 79), a *shofar*, a messenger dispatched from radiant regions (pp. 155–156), a kind of revitalizing drug (p. 119)—in short, the long-awaited knight who holds out for the heroine new hope. But like Mrs. Sololow and Mrs. Amsterdam, Mrs. Talmor is both attracted to and wary of this enchanting man, and the relationship that unfolds between them shares much in common with the zigzagging pattern we noted in the pseudoeuphoric stories of *Under One Roof*. A close examination of the text reveals that Noa's most intense expressions of love for Philip remain unexpressed and occur when Philip is either absent or about to leave. Shortly before his departure back to Britain, Mrs. Talmor addresses Philip internally thus: "But I do not know anything. Only you. I do not see anything. Only you. I do not remember anything. Only your shape. The shape of a man who is like a bright winter day" (p. 123).

Yet when Philip tries to make the least overture towards Mrs. Talmor, (for example, during their trip to Eilat), she rejects him. "He was talking into her face, into her eye, above her lip. But she pressed the door handle, opened to go out. Philip held on to her, pulled her, returned to him. But she opened wide the car's door and went out" (p. 94). Similarly, during their only night together in Tel Aviv, Mrs. Talmor is unable to accept the simple joy of sharing Philip's company and carrying on a simple conversation with him. She keeps asking herself "what went wrong" (pp. 110, 111) and wonders if it is the impact of Tel Aviv, the prosaic city, the city whose pedestrian, pragmatic rhythms remind her of her life in it, the proximity of her house, her obligations, her inescapable social status: "When the spring of possibilities has run dry, the molds are already imposed. And you have nothing else to do but to slip into your set square" (p. 110). However, she will miss bitterly this one night with Philip later on, when, crying, she will tell Mr. Rothman that Philip, obeying her instructions, knelt and said, "Noa, honey, I love you" (p. 134).

That Mrs. Talmor continues to be Noa, that she still desires "to be at the top," becomes clear when she rejects the possibility of settling for a simple friendship with Philip: "She thought: How did I not realize that the answer can be perfectly simple. That the answer for the small days can be: fondness. That is all. Fondness is not silk. It is a common cloth . . . How did I not know. And she answered to herself: How did I not know? Because silk is worth gold, while the cloth that is allegedly so common does not and never did exist . . . The desire to be at the top, and to never stop at less" (p. 97). Mrs. Talmor cannot settle for less than romantic love, just as the demoted princess Anastasia Romanov, with whom the heroine identifies, would probably not accept substitutes for gold or silk.[4] When Philip comes to visit Mrs. Talmor in her Tel Aviv house shortly before his departure to Britain, she repeats in an internal monologue addressed to him her commitment to accept no substitutes for love: "No, Philip, the desire is to be at the top and to never stop at less" (p. 120). But the desire to be at the top with Philip is just as unrealizable as her desire to always be at the top with Asher.

Like in Kahana-Carmon's other pseudoeuphoric stories, Mrs. Talmor's platonic and romantic relationship with Philip leads ultimately to separation. The heroine realizes that the magic is gone when Philip, en route to Iran, visits Israel after the 1967 war. Like Tirtsa and Enokh in "From the Sights of the Stairs Painted Light Blue," and like Yehoshua and Hava in "On the Street," both Mrs. Talmor and Philip understand that they can no longer recreate the unique relationship they shared in the past. Philip stresses that he "did not take into consideration that everything changed so much" (p. 147), while Mrs. Talmor seems to make light of their first encounter: " 'Philip, you and I,' laughed Mrs. Talmor, 'you and I, if one stops to think about it, all in all, just a single night and not the most successful one on the Jaffa beach. Years ago' " (p. 148). However, Mrs. Talmor's attempt to minimize the significance of her encounter with Philip cannot disguise her pain.

Following Philip's departure, Mrs. Talmor tries to adapt herself to a more pragmatic script and to undertake a socially sanctioned "productive" and successful activity. She begins to create decorative mobiles in an attempt to "signal, to convey to the outside what was absorbed in her from the outside" (p. 158). Despite the popularity of her handiwork, she realizes that this occupation is no more than a substitute. "One day she took a stick. With wrath she threw her mobiles to the floor, trampled [them]: wretched mobiles, ridiculous, wretched mobiles" (p. 159). Since the mobiles constitute a suggestive metaphor, it is not entirely clear what Mrs. Talmor is trying to destroy. Is she demolishing her hopes for pro-ductive work? For self-assertion? Were the mobiles meant to substitute for the goals she had as Noa, or for her relationship with Philip? As decorative objects throwing interlacing patterns of light and shade on the wall (p. 23), the mobiles are to some extent symbolic of her shifting moods. On the other hand, I tend to agree with Galit Hasan-Rokem who argues that, for the heroine, the mobiles represent only forms: "[These forms have no intrinsic meaning. They are the debris of their creatrix's disappointment and sorrow."[5]

But, true to Kahana-Carmon's pseudodysphoric plot, the heroine's rebellion leads to no dramatic, visible disaster. Unlike Amos Oz's Eva Harish, Mrs. Talmor does not flee her home, and unlike A.B. Yehoshua's Naomi, she does not go mad. At the same time, however, she finds no way out of her predicament. Her solution is resignation, the price of which is increasing apathy. Her husband, who is aware of the exterior aspects of her deterioration contrasts her present "indifferent face" with her past attractiveness and popularity. This is how he presents it to their daughter, Gavriela: "Mother was a star. It was good, it was wonderful, to be around her. There were always people around her; everyone wanted her. And she was vivacious, smart, cute, unpredictable, a happy and curious person. Could you believe it?" (p. 158).

But just how are we to understand Mrs. Talmor's predicament? Are we to infer that she is a victim of a wayward desire to be at the top, or of patriarchal arrangements which a priori undermine such desires? Is Mrs. Talmor's desire to be at the top a basic, human, necessary need to experience life to the fullest, or is it the product of an infantile weakness (as Asher would have it)? How are we to interpret her tragedy: as the necessary demise of a romantic, or as an implicit indictment of a male-dominated society? Does the novel validate or question the heroine's desire to be at the top? Does it valorize or deplore the heroine's withdrawal into her self? Does the novel affirm romantic love, or does its combination of pseudoeuphoric and pseudodysphoric plots signal a criti-que of the false promise of traditional romance? Does the novel question the heroine's retreat into herself, or does it celebrate it as the female Other's only weapon?

And Moon in the Valley of Ajalon does not offer simple or unilateral answers to these questions. It would seem that the heroine's desire to be at the top is both wrongheaded and noble. Similarly, her retreat into herself is presented both as an escape from a male-dominated world and a self-defeating solution. Mrs. Talmor's resignation is lamented as an unfortunate result of a male-dominated world—unfortunate and inevitable. The novel explains her social isolation, but does not lose sight of its price. Romantic heterosexual love is both celebrated and exposed as an illusion. What the novel implies with less ambiguity is that Mrs. Talmor's predicament is universal. The intense subjectivity which typifies *And Moon in the Valley of Ajalon* must not obscure its concern with the female predicament in general.

The Female Predicament

Mrs. Talmor's monologues reveal the extent to which the heroine understands her predicament as the unavoidable fate of all women. At one point she says to Philip: "Every married woman, something is broken in her. Or she is a hard woman" (p. 40). Mrs. Talmor thinks of herself as "the average Israeli woman" (p. 82). The numerous analogies between the heroine and her friends Bruria and Yemima seem to validate her perceptions.[6]

Both Bruria and Yemima are socially isolated, and especially alienated from their respective husbands, Iov and Nahman. Twenty years after she gives up her artistic aspirations and moves to Iov's provincial village, Bruria finds herself communicating with him via mail because he is engaged in business trips that take him as far away as Peru (pp. 144–147). Unlike Bruria, Iov does not appear to be willing to sacrifice his career for the sake of his marrige. Iov's tendency to put lucrative considerations before relationship with his wife parallels the same tendency in Asher Talmor. The profligate Nahman, on the other hand, can be read as Asher's foil, bringing out with greater intensity how Asher's affair with his secretary Sonia might have affected Mrs. Talmor. Both Iov and Nahman can in fact be read as intensified versions of Asher, especially with respect to the latter's dismissive treatment of his wife.

Bruria's loneliness and Yemima's imposed celibacy (Nahman is too busy with other women, pp. 163–177) parallel the heroine's predicament. The simpler mythogynies of her foils bring out with greater intensity the inevitibility of the heroine's trajectory. Like Mrs. Talmor, Yemima enjoys a short platonic love affair with the attractive Dr. T., who supervises her hysterectomy. As a metaphor for her loss of reproductive and (in her case) sexual capabilities, Yemima's hysterectomy embodies the heroines' imposed defeminization. This powerful metaphor also bespeaks the fate of all postmenopausal women in a patriarchal economy. Victimized by a double standard condemning in older women what it applauds in older men, all three women are locked in stultifying marriages with no hope of escaping.

The only one who attempts to escape the prison of patriarchal marriage is Tehila, the heroine of a story which Rothman, Asher's associate, tells Mrs. Talmor one sultry afternoon in Be'er Sheba. Having left her husband and children for another man with whom she is coauthoring a book, Tehila ends up in an insane asylum after a series of sordid affairs with additional men (pp. 134–142). The end of Tehila, who dared realize the dream shared by all three women—that of economic independence, intellectual achievement, and romance—suggests that in patriarchy there is indeed no exit out of the female condition. It implies that for traditional women, marriage is a prison house, but freedom is a madhouse. Damned if she stays married and damned if she escapes, denigrated as a "mere" mother or wife and suspect as a divorcee, traditional woman in patriarchal societies is doomed to experience life as a series of foreclosures. As Mrs. Talmor concludes:

> In advance, the alternatives were limited. The woman stayed. And she does not know why. And she does not know what she lost because of it. But it was all that she had. And you, look at what you did with me. Are you satisfied? Happy? Or: I am Yemima. A hard woman—defeated. Or: I am Tehila. The woman who lost her mind. And Bruria? Ah, Bruria, enchanted Bruria. We are all with you, the girl with the Chinese eyes who was intended to mature slowly and be prepared for something that is supposed to happen, and that never happens (p. 186).

The multiple references to other victimized women ("or" represents various versions of the same story) reinforce the critical implications of the novel's analogic structure. These references intensify certain aspects of the heroine's condition in particular, even as they highlight the universality of the female predicament. The complaint of the anonymous woman Mrs. Talmor overhears one day on a Tel Aviv street echoes her own sad recognition of her stunted life: "My life stopped at the age of twenty-two. The boy was born. Then, the girl. And the little one. Now already in the army. But either way, twenty-three, twenty-four . . . thirty-four . . . forty-four . . . as a tree to which no rings were added" (p. 144). The metaphor of the aging tree which becomes larger without growing captures the oppressiveness entailed in a woman's single-minded devotion to her reproductive role. The nameless woman describes her life as a corrosive passage of time and her emptiness as the result of her duty to nurture others.

Though most of the female characters in the novel are portrayed as middle-class wives and mothers, patriarchal oppression is not limited to them only. The description of the Bedouin woman Mrs. Talmor encounters outside a Be'er Sheba restaurant suggests that women of less privileged classes and races share essentially the same predicament. The dark colors of the black woman's skin, her clothes, her baby, and her hen turn her into the novel's most poignant metaphor of the female predicament: "I am night. [I am] of the earth, refuse and dust. In a metal nose ring, the mouth covered up, and as if without eyes a swollen face: an animal-woman. A black Sudanese. In black Bedouin clothes and a black baby, laying before her a black hen, is crouching to wait outside on the sidewalk. A man is born to toil, and a woman like me to be forgotten" (p. 133). The self-lamentation of the black woman speaks for Mrs. Talmor as well, for despite the difference in their status, both are barred entrance into male-dominated circles of symbolic power. In the Bedouin woman's case, the forbidden space is the restaurant where her husband is playing cards with his friends; in the case of Mrs. Talmor, it is the exclusive club in Eilath where Asher is about to initiate a business deal (pp. 90–94). Both women yield to the males' successful attempt to edge them out. The Bedouin woman waits patiently for her husband in the heat and dust of the city, just as Noa consents to always take the back seat in her husband's car. Though Mrs. Talmor belongs to a more affluent class, she nevertheless remains penniless when her husband forgets to leave her the usual allotment, forcing her to beg Sonia, his lover and secretary, for a loan (pp. 11–14).

Mrs. Talmor, who is no feminist, interprets her demise as an inevitable part of woman's condition. To her, her own and her friends' predicament is not a product of a patriarchal system, but rather of the female condition—an unavoidable universal malaise. Her conclusion, therefore, is that she must resign herself to her loss, and "to do it with equanimity, with balance, with patience" (p. 185). She sees the "obligation to tear yourself away from yourself . . . the loss of options" (p. 185) as an inevitable part of life. She understands the gap between woman's desire for fulfillment and her actual experience as the unbridgeable chasm separating dream from reality: "Why are not things in reality as [when] they were a dream" (p. 185). She is facing with courage and bitterness what she thinks is the only possible solution to her predicament. As she says in her sarcastic response to Yemima's question: "Erred? . . . I do not know if we erred. Simply, one small detail they did not divulge to us: all that we were supposed to live for, one must live without" (p. 185).

There is something unsettling about the heroine's preference for resignation, though it is also in some sense seductive. I would like to suggest that the heroine's resignation should be read as an implicit protest against the patriarchal constraints that are shown to inspire it. For one thing, the gynographic act itself presents a challenge to a literary tradition long dominated by men. By opting to tell the story of a silenced woman, Kahana-Carmon is challenging the androcentric presumption that would identify silence with blankness or weakness. The gynographic resignation inscribes, then, an implicit critique of a system that would silence a creative mind like Mrs. Talmor's. To the extent that the novel insists on male domination as the source of female victimization, it implies an incisive critique of patriarchy. The analogic structuring of the novel's key mythogynies reinforces this reading.

It is therefore curious to note the general critical obliviousness to this point. What we find in the various readings of the novel is either an attempt to deny its focus, or an attempt to contest the validity of that focus. Gershon Shaked's references to the novel's interest in the "war between the sexes" diffuses the urgency and specificity of the problem Kahana-Carmon is addressing and fails to articulate the uniqueness of her perspective.[7] Though Shaked notes the mythogynous analogies in the novel, he does not articulate their thematic function. Instead, he uses them as exemplifications of the novel's unique structure.[8] Shimon Sandbank denies the significance of the novel's perspective by insisting that the heroine is exceptional and therefore lacks the power of a "universal" character. Instead of examining the ideational or aesthetic meaning of what he calls the heroine's "eccentricity," Sandbank tends to dismiss it. According to him, Mrs. Talmor is "no more than the sum total of her strange reactions, " and as such not worthy of our attention.[9] Like most other critics, Sandbank lavishes praise on Kahana-Carmon's technical virtuosity, while at the same time lamenting her failure to address substantial, universal (male?) concerns. In apparent contrast, Avraham Balaban contests the validity of the novel's insight into the female predicament. He argues that Kahana-Carmon's novel "is not convincing in the existential validity of this difference [between modern married men and women]."[10]

The critical procedures noted here remind me of Asher Talmor's misreadings of Noa Talmor. For instead of attempting to decode her gynographic cryptograms, Kahana-Carmon's androcentric critics treat them as "an annoying discomfort. To minimize [it] as much as possible, one must first contain its disturbance [in compliance with] the normal flow of things, and to restrict it" (*And Moon in the Valley of Ajalon*, p. 91).

By containing "the disturbance" created by [androcentric] flow of things," the abovementioned critics minimize the "annoying discomfort" it produced. By putting it in the wrong context, by denying the validity of its insights, by declaring its heroine as "eccentric," androcentric Hebrew critics would have us believe that Kahana-Carmon—much like her protagonist—is other.

The failure of most critics to appreciate the significance of Mrs. Talmor's difference testifies to the male-centered rigidity of the norms which are currently policing the Hebrew literary scene. For even a cursory comparison of A.B. Yehoshua's and Amos Oz's gyniconologies on the one hand and Kahana-Carmon's on the other should be able to make clear the consensual arbitrariness which governs what has come to be known as authenticity. As Nancy K. Miller points out, the authenticity of a female character is for the most part determined by the extent to which she fits traditional literary conventions or maxims: "If no maxim is available to account for a particular piece of behavior, that behavior is read as unmotivated and unconvincing . . . A heroine without a maxim, like a rebel without a cause, is destined to be misunderstood."[11]

The critical dismissal of Mrs. Talmor as eccentric (that is, inauthentic, implausible) derives from an androcentric set of maxims which would deny female protagonists literary heroism. The same set of maxims would deny a female author the legitimacy it unquestioningly bestows on a male author. This phenomenon may explain why Amos Oz's gyniconologies have been accepted as convincing while Amalia Kahana-Carmon's have not. The judgment of Mrs. Talmor as eccentric and of Hana Gonen as authentic teaches us little about female nature and much about the androcentric norms which continue to govern the Hebrew critical establishment. These norms have become so pervasive that they are invisible. In what follows, I question the validity of these norms by undertaking a comparative study of Amalia Kahana-Carmon's Mrs. Talmor and Amos Oz's Hana Gonen.

Noa Talmor and Hana Gonen: A Female-Authored Heroine Meets her Male-Authored Counterpart

At first glance, Noa Talmor and Hana Gonen share much in common. Both are middle-class wives and mothers who are socially isolated and disenchanted with their marriages. Like the demoted queen of romance, both hope to be rescued from their marital prison by a knight, a version of whom both meet—and lose—in the course of the novel. Unable to escape their uxorial and maternal roles, both retreat into their selves. Both heroines are the narrators of their own stories, and are characterized mostly through their internal monologues and evaluated through female analogues, male foils, and subtle references to Israel's psychohistory. Yet while Noa Talmor emerges as a heroic victim, Hana Gonen emerges as a dangerous victimizer.

The main reason for this distinction lies in the extent to which the narrator-protagonist's point of view is validated by the authorial perspective. While Hana Gonen's perspective on her life is thoroughly discredited by the relentlessly ironic implied author, Noa Talmor's point of view is validated by a thoroughly sympathetic one. For example, because *My Michael* offers few and rather unimpressive details about Hana Gonen's premarital life, it is difficult to justify her tendency to blame her marriage for her demise. The few details the novel does offer about her childhood present her as a domineering young girl who lords it over her Palestinian playmates Halil and Aziz, a part-time auditor at the Hebrew University, and a disinterested kindergarten teacher. *And Moon in the Valley of Ajalon* on the other hand, describes in greater detail the single Noa as a serious, sensitive, and bright student, and an enthusiastic volunteer of impeccable moral integrity to the Palmah. This description lends validity to Mrs. Talmor's complaints, dramatizing with poignancy the destructive impact of her stultifying marriage. Nissim Calderon argues that the novel is not convincing in the characterization of Noa Talmor because it does not offer enough information on the intervening years. In my opinion, since the novel is mostly interested in the tragic contrast between the single Noa and the married Mrs. Talmor rather than in the gradual transformation of the former into the latter, the intervening years, which are normally evoked in the course of the novel, do not have to be sketched out in detail.[12]

From Amos Oz's dismissive treatment of Hana's premarital life, it is not difficult to conclude that her demise is the product of an *inherently* discontented temper. Kahana-Carmon's insistence on the contrast between Noa and Mrs. Talmor, on the other hand, makes it clear that her heroine's predicament is the result of her failed marriage. Whereas Mrs. Talmor's complaint is validated by the characterization of Asher Talmor as a callous opportunist, Mrs. Gonen's complaint is undermined by the characterization of Michael as an understanding and loving husband. Hana despises Michael because he fails to reach the heroic stature of the legendary Michael Strogoff, her childhood hero. She resents her husband for his failure to satisfy her sadomasochistic cravings. Mrs. Talmor, on the other hand, is disenchanted with her husband's transformation from an idealistic young man into a greedy pragmatist. Hana

Gonen cannot come to terms with society because her expectations, inspired for the most part by fiction and romance, are unrealistic. Mrs. Talmor prefers social isolation because she refuses to compromise her principles by joining the capitalistic race for power and status.

There is therefore in Mrs. Talmor something of the demoted queen, that vulnerable and tragic heroine we met in *Under One Roof*, who is unredeemable even by the most noble of knights. Mrs. Talmor rejects Philip's overtures even at the height of her passionate attachment to him mostly because, like Princess Anastasia, she refuses to settle for substitutes. She will not compromise her desire to be at the top. Clandestine, adulterous affairs are beneath her dignity. This may explain why her most passionate addresses to Philip remain unarticulated, or rather unvoiced. The inner world of the heroine reveals her as tragically majestic, as a queen in rags.

The royal image has a distinctly different function in the characterization of Hana Gonen. Her belief in her identity as a queen reveals a megalomaniacal thirst for power. Her internal dialogues with her imaginary lovers disclose an unmistakable sadomasochistic desire to oppress and be oppressed by them. While Mrs. Talmor's internal dialogues with Philip reflect the intensity of her love and pain, Hana Gonen's internal monologues disclose her pathetic confusion of love with aggression. Consequently, the image of the queen serves to satirize the heroine's self-delusions and misplaced sense of superiority.

But it is Hana's inner world in its totality rather than her social and marital context, that finally indicts her. Teeming with images of violence and sexual perversion, this inner world deprives the heroine's retreat into her self of moral justification. By contrast, the juxtaposition of Mrs. Talmor's inner world, rich with perceptive insights, poetic intensity, and informed by high-minded principles, validates psychological escape from a lackluster world of humdrum rountines and questionable procedures.

Whereas in *My Michael*, as we have seen in Chapter 4, the major function of such analogous gyniconologies as Aunt Genia and Mrs. Glick is to highlight aspects of Hana's mental sickness, in *And Moon in the Valley of Ajalon* analogous gyniconologies serve to highlight the destructive impact of patriarchal constraints. Bruria, Yemima, and Tehila are victims of oppressive marriages, not of defects inherent in their female nature. The opposite is true of *My Michael*. Amos Oz's mentally and physically sick women exemplify different possible versions of a middle-aged Hana. Because there is no explanation for the degeneration of Hana, Genia, or Mrs. Glick, it is tempting to associate their degeneration with their femininity, or even to see in their femininity the major cause of their diseases. Kahana-Carmon's analogous mythogynies make a statement about the female *condition*. Amos Oz's novel, on the other hand, implies that women's malaise is a result of an inherent disorder.

For, as we have seen, Hana is bent not only on destroying herself but Michael and Yair a well. Not only does she show no interest in the fate of her drafted husband during the Sinai War, but she is indifferent to war— or,a for that matter, to the nations' welfare in general. Her violent phantasies of dominating Halil and Aziz make it clear that this indifference does not stem from pacifist principles or from a political sympathy with the Arabs. Hana's fantasies of dispatching Halil and Aziz on a terrorist mission present her as a clandestine national enemy. This capacity complements and parallels her adulterous tendencies.

National politics and topography also figure in Kahana-Carmon's novel, but in a significantly different way.[13] The 1948 War of Independence, in which Noa participates as a wireless technician for the Palmah, coincides with Noa's premarital affair with Asher Talmor. Jerusalem is the site of her nascent love for Asher and her dreams for a glorious future: "A new era. Jerusalem. A city in the sky. Here I am in a constant state of slight dizziness . . . . In the spring, there [is] the ultimate [literally most] spring: blue skies, a green-light blue field" (p. 43). As a disillusioned Tel Aviv middle-class wife, the heroine will remember with nostalgia and bitterness the spring in Jerusalem: "Perhaps because this is Tel Aviv, she thought. When the spring of options [is] dried up, the patterns [are] already imposed. And you have nothing else to do but to mechanically slide into your set square" (p. 110). The deterioration of the heroine's marriage corresponds to her topographical transition from Jerusalem to Tel Aviv, which parallels the historical development of Israel from a settlement of idealists into a fragmented bourgeois society. The site of Mrs. Talmor's first meaningful encounter with Philip is Eilath, the developing town which, despite it touristic features, is described as an open place fraught with possibilities. The aftermath of the 1967 Six Days War, which put to rest idealistic dreams of a national return to the prestate era of solidarity and voluntarism, is the background for Mrs. Talmor's last, deeply disenchanting meeting with Philip. The heroine's foreboding suspicion that her special relationship with Philip will not last is conveyed through a series of topograms: "Eilath will become Be'er Sheba. Be'er Sheba will become Tel Aviv. Tel Aviv will become a metropolis" (p. 22).

Mrs. Talmor is an outsider because she would not compromise her social and national ideals in exchange for acceptance. Her alienation from society reveals her commitment to the original ideals of the Yishuv. The differene between her and Hana Gonen, who is presented a a national Other, is considerable. In Kahana-Carmon's novel, there is no oppositional relationship between the heroine's romantic interests and those of the state. Mrs. Talmor despises her husband, not because he is a law-abiding citizen—which is why Hana Gonen hankers after the wild terrorists—but because Asher Talmor's pragmatism makes a mockery of the ideals of socialist Zionism. Unlike Hana Gonen, who dreams of wreaking havoc on Jerusalem, the symbolic locus of national sovereignty—Noa Talmor retreats into her self because she refuses to give up her image of Jerusalem as "a city in the sky."

The thematic correspondence between the country's historical and topographical representation and the heroine's biography enriches both the national and the personal points of reference. The topographies of Jerusalem, Tel Aviv, Eilath, Be'er Sheba, or Metula can be read as metonymic representations of the heroine's changing moods and states of mind. These moods gain the reader's attention because of their vitality and complexity, not because of their "symbolic" meaning. Kahana-Carmon's gynography avoids mythogynous symbolizations and opts instead for precision and complexity. The globalized mythogynies of Oz, on the other hand, invite the reader to speculate about their possible allegorical functions. I would suggest that the reason for the various allegorical readings of *My Michael* lies in the novel's globalizing, arbitrary mythogynies. By resorting to the Arab-Israeli conflict as the real theme of the novel, critics have managed to explain and dignify the novel's stereotypic gyniconologies. Ironically, however, because *And Moon in the Valley of Ajalon* does not lend itself to easy symbolizations, its focal mythogyny has been faulted as "wasted on the peripheral."

Toward a Conclusion:
The Woman Author as Other

Amalia Kahana-Carmon's interest in the denotational and connotational rather than the symbolic aspects of her heroines may explain their perceived Otherness. The author's focus on her heroine's consciousness and conscience defies the androcentric tendency of her male counterparts to objectify female identity. This may explain why androcentric critics have declared Kahana-Carmon's Gynographies as other.

I would like to suggest that the critical attitude to Amalia Kahana-Carmon signals an entrenched, though widely unnoticed, tendency in Hebrew criticism to trivialize female-centered gynographies. Amos Oz's *My Michael*, for example was also criticized, but it was never indicted as peripheral or esoteric. Rachel Eytan's *In the Fifth Heaven*, Miriam Schwartz's *The Story of Eve Gotlieb*, Ruth Almog's *The Stranger and the*

plays. There is no necessary contradiction between Zvulun's creativity and consuming love for Wendy Otis, the ambitious academician. For Wendy, however, love and sex are incompatible with career and work. By presenting Wendy Otis as in many ways an opposite of Mrs. Talmor, Kahana-Carmon appears to subscribe to the patriarchal dichotomizing of femininity and professional commitment, procreativity and creativity.

In this context, one may consider Carolyn Heilbrun's observation about the general reluctance of women novelists to present fictively their own struggles and accomplishments: "Yet woman writers . . . have been unable to imagine for other women, fictional or real, the self they have in fact achieved."[15] It may be that Kahana-Carmon's tendency to avoid combining sexual and emotional maturity and creativity in a heroine (Neima Sasson is a prepubescent girl) stems not only from a literary tradition which tends to identify creativity with masculinity. The tendency of Israeli women authors to avoid such mythogynies, may stem from the foreknowledge that their presentations of women as authors may be indicted as confessional or autobiographical—that is, derivative. As Kahana-Carmon puts it, in Hebrew literary tradition, the biography of Mrs. Pencil will always be considered as secondary, as far less significant than that of Mr. Pencil (see introduction in chapter 5).

In *Magnetic Fields*, which focuses in three different but related stories on the theme of progressive shifts in one's scale of priorities, Kahana-Carmon seems to move beyond the image of male-dependent woman. Wendy Otis in "There is the News Room", is an ambitious American historian who, as she puts it, is "married" to her research work.[16] Wendy's encounter in London with Zvulun Leipzig does not change her life or set of priorities. After three weeks of close (mostly platonic) relationship with Zvulun, she disappears. Narrated from Leipzig's point of view, the story details his attempt to recapture the magic of their relationship, why and how it turned Wendy into the center of his life, and why and how it ended. Perceiving Wendy as "an angel disguised as a human being" (p. 75), Leipzig does not become vindictive, violent, or resentful, as his likely counterparts would in male-authored works. Rather, he lets himself experience the joy and the pain produced by his discovery of and separation from Wendy. Despite his pain, the protagonist-narrator realizes that Wendy taught him much about himself, his strengths and vulnerabilities. He understands that Wendy catalyzed his transition from one magnetic field to another—from a preoccupation with his creative work to an interest in people and the anatomy of interpersonal relationships.

As I already noted, *Magnetic Fields* did not fare as well with the critics as did Kahana-Carmon's previous works. One wonders to what ex-

tent this ambiguous critical reception is related to the innovative
mythogyny the book introduced. Nissim Calderon, for example, condemns Wendy as a cardboard character.[17] Instead of pointing out the innovativeness of the character, Imanuel Berman, who defends Wendy
against such accusations, notes that she is to a large extent an extension
of Kahana-Carmon's male characters.[18] But why is it necessary to
perceive Wendy as a male character in disguise? Why should a
characterization of an ambitious woman who is committed to her work
be perceived as implausible?

On the other hand, one wonders why Amalia Kahana-Carmon
preferred to assign to Wendy a secondary role. I am not sure why
Kahana-Carmon denied Wendy the protagonistic status she gives to
male-dependent women like Mrs. Talmor. For, after all, Wendy's story
remains untold. As Zvulun Leipzig says, "I will never know, I will never
hear her version of the story" (p. 212). I also wonder why Kahana-
Carmon preferred to give this character an American identity. Is it a
coincidence that the independent professional woman is an American,
and that she enchants an Israeli playright in London? Did Kahana-
Carmon feel that she might strain her Israeli readers' suspension of
disbelief by offering us a sympathetic treatment of an ambitious and independent Israeli woman, in Israel?

The story of the Israeli woman as a "liberated" woman remains to be
told in Hebrew narrative fiction. It may not be coincidental that *Magnetic
Fields* ends as a man's love story, much like S.Y. Agnon's novel
Shira (1971). Shira, the independent nurse who has a short affair with
Professor Manfred Herbst and later disappears without any explanation,
becomes in the course of the novel the object of Herbst's obsession,
while Herbst becomes the novel's protagonist. Agnon's typical romantic
irony ("I will not show you Shira, for she has left no trace and no one
knows where she is.") cannot disguise the fact that Shira remains a riddle in the novel.[19]

The scarcity in Hebrew letters of such gyniconologies as Wendy may
be largely related to the small number of women authors who have enjoyed critical attention. It will take more than one or even several women
authors like Kahana-Carmon to change not only the gyniconological
repertoire, but also the literary climate which tends to underestimate
gynographic works, female centered works by women writers.
It will probably take more than one book to change a critical establishment that still tends to dismiss as others women critics, who are interested in literary female others, be they fictional characters or
authors.

Notes

Chapter 1. Introduction

1. See *The New Feminist Criticism: Essays on Women, Literature and Theory* ed. Elaine Showalter (New York: Pantheon, 1985); *Making a Difference: Feminist Literary Criticism* ed. Gayle Greene and Coppélia Kahn (London and New York: Methuen, 1985); *The Female Body in Western Culture: Semiotic Perspectives* a special issue of *Poetics Today* vol. 6/1–2 (1985) ed. Susan Rubin Suleiman; *Gender and Reading: Essays on Readers, Texts, and Contexts* ed. Elizabeth A. Flynn and Patrochinio P. Schweickart (Baltimore and London, The Johns Hopkins University Press, 1986); *The (M)other Tongue: Essays in Feminist Psychoanalytic Interpretation* ed. Shirley Nelson Garner, Claire Kahane and Madelon Sprengnether (Ithaca and London: Cornell University Press, 1985).

2. Nina Auerbach, "Feminist Criticism Reviewed," *Gender and Literary Voice* ed. Janet Todd (New York and London: Holmes and Meier, 1980), p. 258.

3. *On Deconstruction: Theory and Criticism after Structuralism*, Jonathan Culler (Ithaca, New York: Cornell University Press, 1982), p. 46.

4. See for example, *Burning Air and a Clear Mind: Contemporary Israeli Women Poets* ed. Myra Glazer (Athens, Ohio: Ohio University Press, 1981); *Stories of Women of the First Aliya* [Sipurei nashim benot ha'aliya harishona] ed. Yafa Berlowitz (Tel Aviv: Tarmil, 1984); Esther Fuchs, "The Beast Within: Women in Amos Oz's Early Fiction," *Modern Judaism* vol. 4/3 (1984), pp. 311–321; "The Sleepy Wife: A Feminist Consideration of A.B. Yehoshua's Fiction," *Hebrew Annual Review* vol. 8 (1984), pp. 71–81; "Women as Traitors in Israeli Fiction: Steps Toward Defining the Problem, *"Shofar* 4/1 (Fall, 1985), pp. 5–16; "Images of Love and War in Contemporary Israeli Fiction: Toward a Feminist Revision," *Modern Judaism* vol. 6/2 (May 1986), pp. 189–196. Yael S. Feldman, "Inadvertent Feminism: the Image of the Frontier Woman in Contemporary Israeli Fiction," *Modern Hebrew Literature*, vol. 10/3–4 (Spring/Summer 1985), pp. 34–37.

5. See "A New Opening, "[Petiha hadasha] *Hasifrut* vol. 1 no. 1 (33) (Summer, 1984), p. 9. This and all the following references to Hebrew sources are based on my translations.

6. See for example, *The Prism of Sex: Essays in the Sociology of Knowledge* ed. Julia a. Sherman and Evelyn Torton Beck (Madison: University of Wisconsin Press, 1979).

7. The Hebrew subtitle of *Hasifrut* is "A Journal for the Science of Literature."

8. "Feminism and Science," *Feminist Theory: A Critique of Ideology* ed. Nannerl O. Keohane, Michelle Z. Rosaldo, and Barbara C. Gelpi (Chicago: The University of Chicago Press, 1982), pp. 113–126.

9. For a short history of the Israeli Women's Movement, see Natalie Rein, *Daughters of Rachel: Women in Israel* (London and New York: Penguin, 1979), pp. 101–160.

10. "Poetics and Politics: Israeli Literary Criticism Between East and West," *Proceedings of the American Academy for Jewish Research* vol. 52 (1985), p. 34.

11. See for Example, *Major Trends in Contemporary Hebrew Prose: Tales of Experience* [Megamot besiporet hahoveh] ed. Hillel Barzel (Tel Aviv: Yachdav, 1979); Dan Miron, *Current Israeli Prose-Fiction: Views and Reviews* [pinkas patuah] (Tel Aviv: Sifriat Poalim, 1979); Nissim Calderon, *In a Political Context* [Beheksher politi] (Tel Aviv: Hakibbutz Hameuchad, 1980).

12. See *Current Israeli Prose-Fiction*, pp. 95; 100.

13. See Yosef Oren, *The Disillusionment in Israeli Narrative Fiction* [Hahitpakhut basiporet ha'israelit] (Tel Aviv: Yachad, 1983).

14. "Brenner's Wife Rides Again," *Moznayim* vol. 59/4 (October 1985), p. 11. For a more detailed discussion see chapter 5.

15. See "Challenges and Question Marks: On the Political Meaning of Hebrew Fiction in the Seventies and Eighties." *Modern Hebrew Literature* (Spring/Summer 1985), vol. 10 nos. 3–4, p. 16.

16. "Challenges and Question Marks," p. 16.

17. For a detailed discussion of the meaning and implications of political criticism see, Terry Eagleton, *Literary Theory: An Introduction* (Minneapolis: University of Minnesota Press, 1983), especially pp. 194–217.

18. See for example, Gershon Shaked, *If You Ever Forget* [Im tishkah ei pa'am] (Tel Aviv: Ecked, 1971). See also Lev Hakak, *Inferior and Superior* [Yerudim vena'alim] (Jerusalem: Kiriat Sefer, 1981). See especially Arnold Band's preface to the book.

19. See "The Kidnapping of Bialik and Tchernichovsky," *After the Tradition: Essays on Modern Jewish Writing* (New York: E.P. Dutton, 1969), pp. 226–240.

20. See Simon Halkin, *Modern Hebrew Literature: From the Enlightenment to the Birth of Israel—Trends and Values* (New York: Schocken, 1970; first edition 1950)."

21. "Afterword: A Problem of Horizons," *Contemporary Israeli Literature* a special volume of *TriQuarterly* 39 (Spring, 1977), p. 326. See also the prefaces to Yehuda Amichai, A.B. Yehoshua and Amos Oz in Robert Alter ed. *Modern Hebrew Literature* (New York: Behrman House, 1975).

22. See, for example, Shimon Sandbank, "Contemporary Israeli Literature: the Withdrawal from Certainty," *Contemporary Israeli Literature*, pp. 3–18.

23. See *Israeli Stories: A Selection of the Best Writing in Israel Today* ed. Joel Blocker with and introduction by Robert Alter (New York: Schocken, 1962). *Eight Great Hebrew Short Novels* eds. Alan Lelchuk and Gershon Shaked (New York: New American Library, 1983). See also *Modern Hebrew Short Stories* ed. Ezra Spicehandler (New York: Bantam, 1971); *New Writing in Israel* eds. Ezra Spicehandler and Curtis Arnson (New York: Schocken, 1976). See also *Modern Hebrew Literature* ed. Robert Alter.

24. *Great Hebrew Short Novels*, p. ix.

25. David Avidan, "Yona Wallach—the Net Value," [Yona Wallach:ha-erekh hanakuv] *Yediot Aharonot* (November 8, 1985), p. 21. "Nakuv" in Hebrew means both "net" and "filled with holes." The misogynous pun is enhanced by the fact that *nekev* is the root of both "nekev" (hole) and "nekeva" (female).

26. See "Poetry as Politics and Politics as Sex" [Shira kepolitika upolitika kemin], *Yediot Aharonot* (December 20, 1985), p. 25.

27. *Yediot Aharonot* (December 20, 1985), p. 25.

28. For a detailed analysis of the concept of the Other and patriarchy in Western culture and literature see *The Second Sex* tr. and ed. H. M. Parshley (New York: Vintage, 1952), especially pp. 157–223. See also Kate Millet, *Sexual Politics*, (New York: Ballantine, 1969), and Luce Irigaray, *Speculum of the Other Woman* tr. Gillian C. Gill (Ithaca, New York: Cornell University Press, 1985).

29. On the limitations of the critical approach that seeks to correlate history or experience with literary images see Toril Moi, *Sexual/Textual Politics: Feminist Literary Theory* (London and New York: 1985), pp. 42–49.

30. I am adapting here Roland Barthes' semiotic analysis of visual images. See "Rhetoric of the Image," *Image- Music- Text* tr. Stephen Heath (New York: Hill and Wang, 1977), pp. 32–51. For a more detailed semiotic analysis of myth see Barthes' *Mythologies* tr. Annette Lavers (New York: Hill and Wang, 1985), pp. 109–159.

31. For a good synthesis of mimetic and functional approaches to character in literary narrative see Shlomith Rimmon-Kenan, *Narrative Fiction: Contemporary Poetics* (London and New York: Methuen, 1983), pp. 29–42; 59–70.

Chapter 2. The Generation of Statehood

1. For a detailed analysis of the New Wave and the shift to the Generation of Statehood, see Gershon Shaked, *A New Wave in Hebrew Narrative Fiction* [Gal hadash ba-siporet ha-ivrit] (Tel Aviv: Sifriat Poalim, 1974). See also Nurith Gertz, *Generation Shift in Literary History: Hebrew Narrative Fiction in the Sixties* [Hirbat hiz'a vehaboker shelemohorat] (Tel Aviv: Hakibbutz Hameuchad, 1983), pp. 9–44.

2. See Baruch Kurzweil, *In Search of Israeli Literature* Hipus hasifrut hayisraelit] (Ramat Gan: Bar Ilan University, 1982), pp. 22–60. Compate Kurzweil' critical response to Shaked's approving criticism in *A New Wave.*

3. For a critique on the literary flight from politics, see Calderon, *In a Political Context.* For a short description of an apparent emergence of a new "concretist" style in Israel fiction, see Dan Miron, *Current Israeli Prose—Views and Reviews* [Pinkas Patuah] (Tel Aviv: Sifriat Poalim, 1979).

4. See my article, "Women as Traitors" pp. 5–16.

5. *Life as a Parable* [Ha'haim kemashal] (Jerusalem and Tel Aviv: Schocken, 1968), p. 137. Chapter 10, which describes the hero's affair with the carnal teenagers Adah and Havah, is entitled "Through the Sewers of Jerusalem."

6. Ibid., p. 458.

7. In some of the works by Aharon Appelfeld, Itamar Yaoz Kest, Shamai Golan, and Sami Michael that focus on the alienation of the Jewish immigrant in the society of native Sabras, the Sabras are female, whereas the victimized hero is male.

8. "A Problem of Horizons," in *Defenses of the Imagination: Jewish Writers and Modern Historical Crisis* (Philadelphia: The Jewish Publication Society, 1977), p. 257.

9. Compare Ehud Ben Ezer, "Milhama umatzor basifrut hay israelit 1967–1976" [War and Siege in Israeli Literature 1967–1976], *Iton 1977* (April–May, 1977), Vol, 1/2 pp 1, 8–9.

10. Kurzweil, *In Search of Israeli Literature*, p. 67.

11. *Himo: King of Jerusalem* [Himo Melekh Yerushalayim] (Tel Aviv: Am Oved, 1966), pp. 170–171.

12. See Sandra M. Gilbert, "Soldier's Heart: Literary Men, Literary Women, and the Great War," *Signs: Journal of Women in Culture and Society* vol. 8, no. 3 (Spring, 1983), pp. 422–450.

13. Amos Oz, *My Michael* [Michael sheli] (Tel Aviv: Am Oved, 1983; first published 1968), p. 178.

14. Amos Oz, *My Michael*, p. 197.

15. For further details, see Nira Yuval-Davis, "Front and Rear: The Sexual Division of Labor in the Israeli Army," *Feminist Studies*, vol. 11, no. 3 (Fall, 1985), pp. 649–675.

16. The association of women with treachery has a long tradition in Western culture and literature. See, for example, H.R. Hays, *The Dangerous Sex: The Myth of Feminine Evil* (New York: G.P. Putnam's Sons, 1964); and Katherine M. Rogers, *The Troublesome Helpmate: A History of Misogyny in Literature* (Seattle and London: University of Washington Press, 1966).

17. Yitzhak Ben Ner, "Nicole," in *Rustic Sunset* [Shkia kafrit] (Tel Aviv: Am Oved, 1976), p. 170.

18. Judith Fetterley points out an analogous attitude to women and sexuality in Hemingway's *Farewell to Arms*. See *The Resisting Reader: A Feminist Approach to American Fiction* (Bloomington and London: Indiana University Press, 1977), p. 51.

19. Ben Ner, "Nicole," p. 179.

20. Ibid., p. 180.

21. Herbert Marcuse, *Eros and Civilization* (Boston: Beacon Press, 1966), pp. 222–236.

22. See David Ben Gurion, *Israel: A Personal History* (New York: Funk and Wagnalls, 1971), quoted in Natalie Rein, *Daughters of Rachel: Women in Israel* (New York: Penguin, 1979), p. 48.

23. Gilbert, "Soldier's Heart," p. 425.

24. Sanday, *Female Power and Male Dominance: On the Origins of Sexual Inequality* (London and New York: Cambridge University Press, 1981), p. 185.

25. René Girard, *Violence and the Sacred*, tr. Patrick Gregory (Baltimore and London: The Johns Hopkins University Press, 1972), pp. 1–39.

26. Yosef Oren, *Hahitpakhut basiporet hayisraelit* [The disillusionment in Israeli narrative fiction] (Tel Aviv: Yachad, 1983).

27. Oren, *The Disillusionment*, p. 24.

Chapter 3. A.B. Yeoshua: The Lack of Consciousness

1. On Yehoshua's progressive shift from symbolism to realism, see Kurzweil, *In Search of Israeli Literature*, pp. 307–318. See also Gershon Shaked, "Was it Only in the Beginning of Summer 1970?" [Haumnam rak bitehilat kayits 1970], *Siman Kri'a*, vol. 1 (1972), p. 150.

2. For a detailed discussion of Yehoshua's poetics of characterization and

his comic writing, see Nilli Sadan-Loebenstein, *A.B. Yehoshua* (Tel Aviv: Sifriat Poalim, 1981), pp. 124–127.

3. For a detailed discussion of Yehoshua's break from the Palmah Generation, see ibid., pp. 9–22; and Gertz, *Generation Shift in Literary History*, pp. 177–204.

4. See A.B. Yehoshua, *Between Right and Right* [Bizekhut hanormaliut] (Tel Aviv: Schocken, 1980), pp. 55–62.

5. On the stereotype of female passivity and mindlessness in Western literature, see Mary Ellmann, *Thinking About Women* (New York: Harcourt Brace Jovanovich, 1968), pp. 55–146.

6. For a similar theory, see Mary Allen's study of American narrative fiction in *The Necessary Blankness: Women in Major American Fiction of the Sixties* (Urbana: University of Illinois Press, 1976).

7. See Alter, *Modern Hebrew Literature*, p. 353. For an allegorical (national) interpretation of Yehoshua's early work, see, for example, Kurzweil, *In Search of Israeli Literature*, pp. 307–318. For the same on his later novels, see Oren, *The Disillusionment*, pp. 27–39.

8. I am using Yosef Haefrati's metaphoric description of Yehoshua's secondary characters. See "Some Texts and Pottery" [Ketsat textim vaharasim], *Siman Kri'a*, vol. 1 (1972), p. 156. On this point, see also Amos Oz, "The Hammer and the Anvil" Hapatish vehasandan], *Siman Kri'a*, vol. 10 (1980), p. 127.

9. See *Man's World, Woman's Place: A Study in Social Mythology* (New York: Dell Publishing Company, 1971).

10. In response to a question concerning the marginality of women in his works, Yehoshua said: "I treated female characters with too much respect. I was afraid of failing to understand even their most basic psychology. Perhaps my fear was exaggerated. I think that they scare me less and less." See Menahem Perry and Nissim Calderon, "Writing Prose: A Conversation With A.B. Yehoshua" [Likhtov proza: siha im A.B. Yehoshua], *Siman Kri'a*, vol. 5 (1976), p. 288.

11. *Ad Horef 1974* [Until Winter 1974] (Tel Aviv: Hakibbutz Hameuchad, 1975), p. 37. Further references to stories included in this anthology will appear in the text and will be indicated as *A.D.*

12. *A New Wave*, p. 129.

13. See *The Feminine Image in Literature* (Rochelle Park State: Hayden Book Company, 1973).

14. See Sadan-Loebenstein, *A.B. Yehoshua*, p. 166.

15. "Woman as Outsider," in *Woman in Sexist Society: Studies in Power and Powerlessness*, ed. Vivian Gornick and Barbara K. Moran (New York: New American Library, 1971), p. 137.

16. For a discussion of the stereotyping of this and other characters in the story, see Nissim Calderon, "Flaws in Narrative Fiction" [Kalkalot basiporet], *Siman Kri'a*, vol. 1 (September, 1972), pp. 313–315.

17. *Early in the Summer of 1970* [Bitekhilat kayitz 1970] (Tel Aviv: Schocken, 1972), p. 9. Further references to this narrative will appear in the text.

18. Compare with Ann, the attractive and neurotic American in Yehoshua's play *Last Treatments* [Tipulim Aharonim] (Tel Aviv: Schocken, 1974), and Yehuda's disoriented younger American wife, Connie, in *Late Divorce* [Gerushim me'uharim] (Tel Aviv: Hakibbutz Hameuchad, 1982).

19. *The Lover* [Hame'ahev] (Tel Aviv: Schocken, 1977), p. 148. Further references to the novel will be included in the text.

20. Katherine M. Rogers points out that the numerous variations in world literature on the portrait of the troublesome helpmate stem from the androcentric expectation that a wife's duty is to obey her husband. Any deviation from this plan is bound to draw criticism as selfishness, idleness, or extravagance. See *The Troublesome Helpmate*. See also my article, "The Sleepy Wife: A Feminist consideration of A.B. Yehoshua's Fiction," in *Hebrew Annual Review* vol. 8 (1984), pp. 71–81.

21. On the technique and function of the distorting angle in Yehoshua's characterization, see Sadan-Loebenstein, *A.B. Yehoshua*, pp. 23–29.

22. "A Long Summer Day, His Despair, His Wife and His Daughter" [Yom sharav arokh, ye'usho ishto ubito], *Ad Horef 1974* (Tel Aviv: Hakibbutz Hameuchad, 1975), p. 162. The story was first published in *Opposite the Forests* [Mul ha'yearot] (Tel Aviv: Hakibbutz Hameuchad, 1968). Further references to the story will appear in the text.

23. "Secondary Class Citizenship: The Status of Women in Contemporary American Fiction," In *What Manner of Woman?* ed. Marlene Springer (New York: New York University Press, 1977), p. 306.

24. *Between Right and Right* [Bizekhut hanormaliut], (Tel Aviv: Schocken, 1980] pp. 141–167.

25. Adam proves to be the better parent in relation to Yigal, their first-born deaf-mute son. He spends more hours with him and learns to communicate with him: "Interestingly, I used to understand him better than Asya. I developed a special ability for understanding his "words" (p. 77). After Yigal's untimely death, it is Adam who insists on having a second child, despite his growing alienation from Asya (pp. 78–82).

26. *Sex and Character*, (London and New York: W. Heinemann and G.P. Putnam's Sons, 1906; first German edition, 1904), pp. 88–89.

27. *Late Divorce* [Gerushim meuharim] (Tel Aviv: Hakibbutz Hameuchad, 1982), p. 80. Further references to this novel will appear in the text.

28. *Sex and Character*, p. 100.

29. For a further discussion of *Late Divorce* from this point of view, see my article, "The Sleepy Wife," pp. 71–81.

30. As Nurith Gertz puts it: "At times she [Vaducha] is a real old woman, and at times she acts and talks like a social or metaphysical symbol." See "Sifrut, hevra, historia" [Literature, Society, History], *Siman Kri'a*, vol. 6 (May, 1979), p. 432.

31. For a detailed allegorical interpretation of Vaducha as the embodiment of the Zionist movement, see Oren, *The Disillusionment*, pp. 35–36.

32. See "The History of the State as a Marriage Story" [Toldot hamedina kesipur nisu'in], *Yediot Aharonot* (July 16, 1982), p. 22. See also my article, "Casualties of Patriarchal Double Standards: Old Women in the Fiction of A.B. Yehoshua," *South Central Bulletin*, vol 43, no. 4 (1984), pp. 107–109.

33. *Sex and Character*, p. 207.

34. "Humanbecoming: Form and Focus in the Neo-Feminist Novel, in *"Images of Women in Fiction: Feminist Perspectives*, ed. Susan Cornillon Koppelman (Bowling Green, Ohio: Bowling Green University Popular Press, 1972), p. 184.

Chapter 4. Amos Oz: The Lack of Conscience

1. *Amos Oz* (Tel Aviv: Sifriat Poalim, 1980), p. 54.

2. *A New Wave*, p. 181.

3. Ibid., p. 47.

4. See, for example, his collection of essays, *Under This Blazing Sun* [Be'or hatkhelet ha'aza] (Tel Aviv: Sifriat Poalim, 1979); and more recently, *A Journey in Israel* [Po vasham be'eretz israel] (Tel Aviv: Am Oved, 1983).

5. *Under This Blazing Sun*, p. 153. See also the essay, "All the Hopes" [Kol hatikvot], pp. 118–124.

6. Amos Elon, *The Israelis: Founders and Sons* (New York: Penguin, 1971).

7. *Amos Oz*, pp. 77, 84.

8. *A New Wave*, p. 184.

9. "The Way of the Wind" [derekh haruah], in *Where the Jackals Howl* [Artsot hatan] (Tel Aviv: Masada, 1965), p. 57.

10. In the revised version of the book (Tel Aviv: Am Oved, 1976), there is a greater emphasis on the kibbutz members' efforts to rescue Gideon. An army officer and an old doctor are brought into the picture. Shimshon Sheinbaum is also somewhat more humanized because he desperately tries to convince Gideon

to jump down. Further references to the original and revised versions will appear in the text with the proper indications of publication dates.

11. Geula Sirkin in "Before His Time" and Tova the poetess in "All the Rivers" are also characterized as repulsive and sex-starved single women. Katherine Rogers points out that the single woman has been a common butt of hostility and derision in world literature; see *The Troublesome Helpmate*, p. 201. See also Dorothy Yost Deegan, *The Stereotype of the Single Woman in American Novels* (New York: King's Crown Press, 1951).

12. In the revised version of the story, Geula has second thoughts about her plot: "How very much she wished to reach a reconciliation and to forgive. Not to hate him and not to wish for his [the Bedouin's] death" (1976, p. 42).

13. See *Amos Oz*, pp. 104–110.

14. This statement also applies to the characterization of Tova the poetess in "All the Rivers," who is consumed by sexual passion and controlled by romantic dreams about marriage. For further details, see my article, "The Beast Within."

15. the idiomatic expression *strange fire* [esh zara] carries strong biblical connotations referring to acts of ritual sacrilege in ancient Israel (e.g., Leviticus 10:1; Number 3:4).

16. Damkov is overcome by passion only after Galila rejects his story, and invites him thus: "I am not yours, I'm sure I'm not yours, I'm sure. I'm blond. I may, we may, now, I can be yours. Blond! Come!" (1965, p. 23). It is noteworthy that while Yair follows Lily much against his better judgment, Galila evinces an unmistakable sexual interest in the muscular Damkov, who may very well have been her father. For further details, see my article, "The Beast Within."

17. *Sex and Character*, p. 91.

18. *Elsewhere Perhaps* [Maqom aher] (Merhavia: Sifriat Poalim, 1966), p. 87. Further references to the novel will appear in the text. The translations are my own.

19. Despite his critique of some aspects of kibbutz life, Oz, himself a member of kibbutz Hulda, is explicit in his commitment to the original ideals of socialist Zionism. See, for example, his article, "The Platform of the Labor Movement" [Tochnit hamit'ar shel tenuat ha'avoda], in *Under This Blazing sun*, pp. 138–141. See also "A Thought on the Kibbutz," pp. 177–179.

20. We should note in this context that while Oz's middle-aged men (Berger, Harish, Damkov) are described as sexually competent and even attractive, middle-aged women like Bronka and Batya Pinsky are not only repulsive, but pathetic in their hope to retain an active sexual life.

21. Compare Gertz, *Amos Oz*, pp. 120–121.

22. Ibid., p. 118.

23. This is apparently why Rami Rimmon fumbles clumsily during his first attempt at making love to Noga, while Noga knows precisely how to behave and what to require. See pp. 62–63.

24. On the literary stereotype of the female formless mind, see Mary Ellmann, *Thinking About Women*, pp. 74–77.

25. Weininger, *Sex and Character*, p. 188.

26. "What Can a Heroine Do? Or why Women Can't Write," in *Images of Women in Fiction*, p. 6.

27. For an explicit critique by Oz of the Sinai War and its impact on his generation, see Gertz, *Generation Shift in Literary History*, pp. 57–58. On the negative impact on socialist Zionist elite groups of the compensation agreement with Germany and similar pragmatic decisions, see pp. 56–57.

28. *Under This Blazing Sun*, p. 213.

29. For a discussion of the unreliable narrator in *My Michael*, see Arnold Band, "The Unreliable Narrator in *My Michael* and *In the Flower of Her Youth*" [Hamesaper habilti meheman be-michael sheli ubi-demi yameha], *Hasifrut*, vol. 3, no. 1, pp. 30–32. For a more detailed discussion of the heroine's self-deception, see Gertz, *Amos Oz*, pp. 122–138.

30. For the literary conventions of the female-centered novel, see, for example, Wendy Martin, "Seduced and Abandoned in the New World: The Image of Woman in American Fiction," in *Woman in Sexist Society*, pp. 329–346. See also Rachel M. Brownstein, *Becoming A Heroine: Reading About Women in Novels* (New York: Penguin, 1982); and Nancy K. Miller, *The Heroine's Text: Readings in the French and English Novel 1722–1782* (New York: Columbia University Press, 1980), especially pp. 149–158.

31. *My Michael* [Michael sheli] (Tel Aviv: Am Oved, 1983; first published 1968), p. 5. Further references to the novel will be included in text.

32. While Ruth is completely unaware of the political reality in which she lives (post–World War II Palestine shortly before the end of the British Mandate), Hillel is intensely involved in current events. As his mother continues to dream of her anti-Semitic native land Poland, Hillel drafts a letter to the high commissioner denouncing the British Mandate.

33. See, for example Rogers, *The Troublesome Helpmate*, p. 263; and Allen, *The Necessary Blankness*, p. 13.

34. See Dorothy Dinnerstein, *The Mermaid and the Minotaur: Sexual Arrangements and Human Malaise* (New York: Harper Colophon, 1976). See also Nancy Chodorow, *The Reproduction of Mothering: Fsychoanalysis and the Sociology of Gender* (Berkeley and Los Angeles: University of California Press), especially pp. 73–76.

35. See "The Dread of Woman," in *Feminine Psychology* (New York and London: Norton, 1967), p. 135. For a psychoanalytic approach to the problem, see the

above article, pp. 133–146. For an anthropological approach, see Carol Ember, "Men's Fear of Sex with Women: A Cross-cultural Study, "*Sex Roles*, vol. 4 (1978), pp. 657–678.

36. See Millet, *Sexual Politics*, pp. 331–469. On the motif of desirable rape in male-authored pornographic literature, see Andrea Dworkin, *Woman Hating* (New York: E.P. Dutton, 1974), pp. 51–90. On the image of woman as sexual victim and victimizer in pornography, see Angela Carter, *The Sadeian Woman and the Ideology of Pornography*, (New York: Harper Colophon, 1978).

37. Here too, there is an implicit attempt to draw on the widely shared belief that women are inevitably masochistic. For a study of this myth, see Paula Caplan, *The Myth of Women's Masochism* (New York: E.P. Dutton, 1985).

38. "Woman as Outsider," p. 131. For an investigation into the male-centered bias underlying "scientific" diagnoses of women as mad, see Phyllis Chesler, *Women and Madness* (New York: Avon, 1972).

39. *The Necessary Blankness*, p. 9.

40. "These [characters] are concretizations of forces in the human spirit, but are not a precise revelation of human characters. The archetypes working in the human spirit are more important than the unique individual." See Shaked, *a New Wave*, p. 184.

41. *Figures II* (Paris: Seuil, 1969), p. 175, quoted in Nancy K. Miller, "Emphasis Added: Plots and Plausibilities in Women's Fiction," *PMLA*, vol. 96, no. 1 (January, 1981), p. 36.

42. "Fictional Consensus and Female Casualties," in *The Representation of Women in Fiction*, eds. Carolyn G. Heilbrun and Margaret R. Higonnet (Baltimore and London: The Johns Hopkins University Press, 1983), pp. 1–18. Further references to this work will appear in the text.

43. After Ruth Kipnis's elopement with a vile British admiral, Hillel, her son, grows up in a kibbutz, and her husband Hans becomes a teaching assistant at the university. See *The Hill of Evil Counsel* [Har ha'etsa hara'ah] (Tel Aviv: Am Oved, 1976), pp. 5–54. Further references to this work will appear in the text.

44. "What Can a Heroine Do?" p. 9.

45. See, for example, Gertz, *Amos Oz*, pp. 122–133.

46. See, for example, "The Petit-Bourgeois Sickness," in *Under This Blazing Sun*, pp. 125–133.

Chapter 5. Gynographic Re-visions: Amalia Kahana-Carmon

1. *Iton 1977*, vol. 9 no. 64–65 (May–June, 1985), p. 5. It would be interesting to examine the wording of the judges' decision as quoted in this source. By opening with a reference to "one great [male] author" who said that "in the short story

. . . almost every word must be completely right," the judges are not only complimenting Kahana-Carmon for her obedience to the rules of her "great" literary fathers, but also hinting that her greatest achievements are in the area of the short story rather than the novel. In addition to stressing Kahana-Carmon's sensitivity to words, the judges say that her writing "knows *intuitively* its wished [goal] and searches and looks for it and often finds it and creates out of it a *delicate filigree* of a story" [my italics]. The implicit references to sensibility and intuition—the agreed-upon staples of "feminine writing"—and the metaphor of "a delicate filigree" (echoing the frills on dresses, the pretty embroideries?) reencode the traditional perception of femininity as well as female art.

2. In a recently published lecture ironically entitled "To Be Wasted on the Peripheral," Kahana-Carmon continues her criticism of the status of the female author in Israel. Among other things, she says: "Her [the female author's] place will be determined by, and she will be complimented for her great writing talent, but not for the contents, for the ideas; because the more the values and questions reflect her own as a woman, the more the mainstream will reject them." *Yediot Aharonot* (September 15, 1985), p. 23.

3. Carmon argued against such an interpretation in her essay, "And Joseph Made Himself Known to his Brothers" [Vayitvada yosef el ehav], *Ma'ariv* (December 16, 1966). Quoted in Abraham Balaban, *The Saint and the Dragon* [Hakadosh vehadrakon] (Tel Aviv: Hakibbutz Hameuchad, 1979), p. 185.

4. See, for example, Shaked, *A New Wave*, pp. 168–179; and Balaban, *The Saint and the Dragon*, pp. 1–50.

5. See, for example, Shimon Sandbank, "To Be Wasted on the Peripheral" [Lehitbazbez al Hatsedadi], *Siman Kri'a*, vol. 1 (1972), pp. 326–328. A typical appreciative gesture towards Kahana-Carmon's "carefully chosen language" (p. 41), closely followed with an impatient dismissal of her "severely confined point of view" (p. 42), can be found in Leon I. Yudkin, "Kahana-Karmon [sic] and the Plot of the Unspoken," *Modern Hebrew Literature*, vol 2, no. 4 (Winter, 1976), pp. 30–42.

6. *The Saint and the Dragon*, pp. 51–133.

7. For an example of the ambivalence with which *Magnetic Fields was accepted*, see Gershon Shaked and Nissim Calderon, " '*Magnetic Fields*': Two opinions" [Sadot magnetiyim:shte deot], *Yediot Aharonot* (March 18, 1977), pp. 38–41. For a mystical interpretation of the story, see Emanuel Berman, "The Desire to Be Sacrificed" [Ergon ha'akeda], *Siman Kri'a*, vol. 7 (1977), pp. 431–436.

8. "To Be Wasted on the Peripheral," p. 23.

9. Ibid. In another published lecture, entitled "To Be a Woman-Author" [Lihyot isha soferet], Amalia Kahana-Carmon satirizes the expectation that women writers who have been barred from privileged male domains write about those domains rather than about the "confined" experiences that in all probability have informed their own lives as second-class citizens. Among other things,

she notes that the woman writer is in a double bind. If she remains loyal to her own experiences as a medusa, she risks being criticized as too limited; if, on the hand, she decides to become a dolphin and "write like a man," she risks being charged with inauthenticity. See *Yediot Aharonot* (March 13, 1984), pp. 20–21.

10. See, for example, Mary Ellmann, *Thinking About Women*, pp. 27–54. On the premises and strategies of androcentric literary criticism, see also Cynthia Ozick, "Women and Creativity: The Demise of the Dancing Dog," in *Woman in Sexist Society*, pp. 431–451; Elaine Showalter, "The Double Critical Standard and the Feminine Novel," in *A Literature of their Own: British Women Novelists from Bronte to Lessing* (Princeton, New Jersey: Princeton University Press, 1977), pp. 73–99; and Joanna Russ, *How to Suppress Women's Writing* (Austin: University of Texas Press, 1983).

11. For a critique of traditional androcentric concepts guiding the formation of literary canons, see Lilian S. Robinson, "Treason Our Text: Feminist Challenges to the Literary Canon," *Tulsa Studies in Women's Literature*, vol. 2, no. 1 (1983), pp. 83–98.

12. *A Room of One's Own* (New York and London: Harcourt Brace Jovanovich, 1957; first published 1929), p. 77.

13. Gnessin, Yizhar, and Virginia Woolf are mentioned by Gershon Shaked as Kahana-Carmon's predecessors, See Shaked, *A New Wave*, p. 168.

14. Baron is criticized by Shaked as addressing a "rather confined thematic world." See *Hebrew Narrative Fiction 1880–1970* [Hasiporet ha-ivrit 1880–1970] (Tel Aviv: Hakibbutz Hameuchad, 1977), p. 453.

15. "Brenner's Wife Rides Again," *Moznayim*, vol. 59, no. 4 (October, 1985), p. 13.

16. My argument for the recognition of a women's literary tradition is inspired by Showalter's *A Literature of Their Own*, especially pp. 3–36.

17. See Gertz, *Generation Shift in Literary History*, pp. 84–86; 108–110.

18. *How to Suppress Women's Writing*, pp. 49–61.

19. "Primary Premises" [Muskalot rishonim], *Under One Roof* [Bikhfifa ahat] (Tel Aviv: Hakibbutz hameuchad, 1977; first published 1966), p. 238. Gershon Shaked was right in his interpretation of the story as a fictional expression of Kahana-Carmon's *ars poetica*. Further references to this work, abbreviated as *Roof*, will appear in the text.

20. The term *strobe light* is inspired by Kahana-Carmon's description in "A Piece for the Stage in the Grand Style" of Rembrandt's typical picture as "always dark, though the darkness is broken by illuminated regions . . . Only the climactic points, where the silent drama of the picture is taking place, only they are at the center of the lighting." *Siman Kri'a*, vol 5 (1976), p. 246. This passage, as well as many others in this piece (pp. 241–272), strikes me as self-referential.

21. *And Moon in the Valley of Ajalon* [Veyareah be'emek ayalon] (Tel Aviv: 1971), p. 201.

22. *Generation Shift in Literary History*, pp. 164–175.

23. For a good introduction to Kahana-Carmon's style, see Shaked, *A New Wave*, pp. 176–179, 220–222. For quick surveys in English on Kahana-Carmon's style, see Warren Bargad, "Elements of Style in the Fiction of Amalia Kahana-Carmon," *Hebrew Annual Review*, vol. 2 (1978), pp. 1–16; and Leon I. Yudkin, "Kahana-Karmon [*sic*] and the Plot of the Unspoken."

24. For the concept of women's revisionary writing I am indebted to Sandra M. Gilbert and Susan Gubar, *The Madwoman in the Attic: The Woman Writer and the Nineteenth-Century Literary Imagination* (New Haven and London: Yale University Press, 1979), especially pp. 3–44. Since Hebrew women writers began to achieve critical recognition only in the twentieth century, their struggles and achievements parallel in *some* ways those of nineteenth century English women writers. Yet, although Gilbert and Gubar's paradigm is helpful, it cannot address all or even most of the specific characteristics of Kahana-Carmon or, for that matter, other Hebrew women writers.

25. For an analysis of the Victorian ideology of female propriety, see Mary Poovey, *The Proper Lady and the Woman Writer* (Chicago and London: The University of Chicago Press, 1984). For a semiotic analysis of the female body (its significance and interpretations) in Western culture, see Susan Rubin Suleiman, "(Re)writing the Body: the Politics and Poetics of Female Eroticism," *The Female Body in Western Culture: Semiotic Perspectives*, vol. 6, nos. 1–2 of *Poetics Today* (1985), pp. 43–65.

26. See, for example, de Beauvoir, *The Second Sex*, pp. 242–252; and Millet, *Sexual Politics*, pp. 333–411.

27. "Yona Wallach–the Net Value", p. 21. Avidan goes on to belittle Wallach's alleged "competition" with women poets thus: "How many distinguished Hebrew women poets were there after all in the twentieth century . . . and how many are there . . .? the race track was consequently not particularly crowded." For a critical response to Avidan's sexist remarks, see Esther Fuchs, "Poetry as Politics, Politics as Sex," p. 25.

28. See Gilbert and Gubar, *The Madwoman in the Attic*; and Margaret Homans, *Women Writers and Poetic Identity* (Princeton, New Jersey: Princeton University Press, 1980).

29. *Women Writers and Poetic Identity*, p. 12.

30. "Brenner's Wife Rides Again," pp. 12–13.

31. As she herself recognizes, the woman author is like a fish whose fins and tail have been cut off: "And the fish is advancing [after they tied its torn tail back to its body], and is making all the turns, and moves. But instead of the harmony in

the motions, and the wonderful graciousness, appears an uncertain, slipping, wretched movement," "Brenner's Wife," p. 13.

32. I am referring here to Rachel Blau DuPlessis's *Writing Beyond the Ending: Narrative Strategies of Twentieth-Century Women Writers* (Bloomington: Indiana University Press, 1985). This book explores the alternative fictions created by women authors in defiance of "the mechanisms of social insertion of women through the family house, the private sphere, and patriarchal hierarchies" (p. xi).

33. See Nathan Zach, *Air Lines: Talks on Literature* (Jerusalem: Keter, 1983), pp. 11–28. In "The Heart of the Summer, the Heart of the Light," Mrs. Bruchin criticizes the proliferation in Israeli fiction of male violence against female "lovers." Among other things, she says: "For me every book has turned into a race against time: when will appear the woman who disgusts the hero?" *Under One Roof*, p. 213.

34. Balaban, *The Saint and the Dragon*, pp. 8–21.

35. Martin Buber, *I and Thou*, tr. Walter Kaufman (New York: Charles Scribner's Sons, 1970), pp. 56–57. Further references to Buber's work will appear in the text.

36. *Love in the Western World*, tr. Montgomery Belgion (New York: Harcourt Brace Jovanovich, 1940).

37. The author defined as "the enchantment with the primordial forces" the principal theme of "High Gambles," two stories published in 1980 (both are included in *Up in Montifer*, 1984). This definition of two stories (which in essence revolve around the lives of heroines who have been badly abused by their male counterparts) seems to adequately describe the central experience in the euphoric stories of *Under One Roof*. See Amalia Kahana-Carmon, "Stories About Enchantment," *Siman Kri'a*, vols. 12–13 (February, 1981), pp. 229–238.

38. My references to Kahana-Carmon's heroines as princesses or queens and to their male partners as knights are inspired by the royal metaphors she uses in her stories and critical pieces. In her description of Rembrandt's paintings, for example, she says: "What we are seeing is some recognition of the simple nobleness and courage of the human condition. You [feminine] are not an angel, I am not an angel. You are not a queen, I am not a king. But you are an angel and a queen, anyway. And I am an angel, and I am a king, nevertheless." "A Piece for the Stage in the Grand Style," pp. 245–246. The terms *euphoric* and *dysphoric* are inspired by Nancy Miller's analysis of major plot paradigms of female-centered novels. See *The Heroine's Text*.

39. Later in the story, her husband not only helps her serve dinner, but also appears to endorse her interpretation of their new life in the new country: "A new life she [the specialist] says. There is no new life. Life is for one time, what can one do? And this is what I wanted to say a long time ago: I too have no other place. I have no other home" (p. 100).

40. See "Persuasion and the Promises of Love," in *The Representation of Women in Fiction*, ed. Carolyn G. Heilbrun and Margaret R. Higonnet (Baltimore and London: the Johns Hopkins University Press, 1983), pp. 152–180.

41. It would make an interesting study to compare Neima Sasson to Rachel Eytan's Maya *In the Fifth Heaven* (1962). This novel also focuses, though in very different ways, on the makings of the artist as a young girl. Here too, what brings out the heroine Maya's awareness of her creativity is her emotional attachment to Yosef, a man much older than her. Edna, the heroine of Yael Medini's novel, *Arcs and Traces* (1977), also shares much in common with Neima Sasson and Maya.

42. See Mary Jacobus, "The Difference of View," in *Women Writing and Writing About Women*, ed. Mary Jacobus (New York: Harper and Row, 1979), p. 14.

43. Rachel M. Brownstein, *Becoming a Heroine: Reading About Women in Novels* (New York: Penguin, 1982), p. 295.

Chapter 6. Self-Conscious Heroism: *And Moon in the Valley of Ajalon*

1. *And Moon in the Valley of Ajalon* [Veyareah be'emek ajalon] [Tel Aviv: Hakibbutz Hameuchad, 1971], p. 116. Further references to the novel will appear in the text.

2. "A Work of Art" [Ma'aseh hoshev], *Siman Kri'a*, vol. 1 [1972], p. 324.

3. In "A Piece for the Stage in the Grand Style," Kahana-Carmon reiterates the idea that, in any relationship, the more complex and sensitive partner is most likely to be victimized. She adds, however, that in the end the weaker partner will emerge victorious, strengthed by his/her initial alienation from power. (pp. 253–254].

4. At one point, addressing Philip, Mrs. Talmor makes explicit her identification with the deposed princess Anastasia of the House of Romanov: "One must understand: it is not me, not my name, not my family. It is only the solemnity, in which [there i] a bit of bleakness, which opens up to absorb the splendor. This, alone is the royal house, only this," (p.94).

5. See her article, "Like a Man Encountered With a Mirror: On *And Moon in the Valley of Ajalon* by Amalia Kahana-Carmon" [Akh keish nitkal bire'i: iyun *beveyareah be'emek ayalon*], *Hasifrut*, vols. 30–31 [April 1981], p. 190.

6. On the analogic technique in the novel, see Shaked, *A New Wave*, pp. 213–216; Calderon, "A Work of Art,; p. 323–326; and Hasan-Rokem, "Like a Man," pp. 184–189.

7. *A New Wave*, pp. 206, 210.

8. *A New Wave*, pp. 213–216.

9. "To Be Wasted on the Peripheral," p. 327.

10. *The Saint and the Dragon*, p. 93.

11. "Emphasis Added: Plots and Plausibilities in Women's Fiction," *PMLA*, vol. 96, no. 1, p. 36.

12. Calderon, "A Work of Art,", pp. 322–323.

13. On the semiotic function of historical and topographical details in the novel, see Shaked, *A New Wave*, pp. 216–219; Balaban, *The Saint and the Dragon*, pp. 101–110; and Hasan-Rokem, " 'Like a Man' "pp. 185–187.

14. " 'Like a Man' ", p. 190. See also Shaked, *A New Wave*, pp. 174–176.

15. Carolyn G. Heilbrun, *Reinventing Womanhood* [New York: Norton, 1979], p. 72.

16. *Magnetic Fields* [Sadot nagnetiyim] (Tel Aviv: Hakibbutz Hameuchad, 1977), p. 53. Further references to this work will appear in the text.

17. " 'Magnetic Fields': Two Opinions," pp. 40–41.

18. "The Desire to be Sacrificed," p. 433.

19. *Shira* (Jerusalem and Tel Aviv: Schocken, 1971), p. 537. On Agnon's romantic irony [and ironic art in genera], see my book, *Cunning Innocence: On S.Y. Agnon's Irony* (Tel Aviv: Tel Aviv University, 1985 in Hebrew), especially pp. 127–155. See also my *Comic Aspects in S.Y. Agnon's Fiction* (Tel Aviv: Reshajim, 1987).

Index